THE ORIGINS OF UNHAPPINESS

THE ORIGINS
OF UNHAPPINESS

A New Understanding of Personal Distress

David Smail

Routledge
Taylor & Francis Group

LONDON AND NEW YORK

First published 1993 by HarperCollins*Publishers*

This edition published in 2015 by Karnac Books Ltd.

Published 2018 by Routledge
2 Park Square, Milton Park, Abingdon, Oxon OX14 4RN
711 Third Avenue, New York, NY 10017, USA

Routledge is an imprint of the Taylor & Francis Group, an informa business

British Library Cataloguing in Publication Data
A C.I.P. for this book is available from the British Library

ISBN: 9781782202875 (pbk)

Contents

Figures

Introduction

In order to develop a view of emotional distress which is both helpful and true, one has, I believe, to turn prevalent understandings inside out. Instead of looking inward to detect and eradicate within ourselves the products of 'psychopathology', we need to direct our gaze out into the world to identify the sources of our pain and unhappiness. Instead of burdening ourselves with, in one form or another, the responsibility for 'symptoms' of 'illness', 'neurotic fears', 'unconscious complexes', 'faulty cognitions' and other failures of development and understanding, we would do better to clarify what is wrong with a social world which gives rise to such forms of suffering.

This is not to say that we are not psychologically and emotionally damaged by our experience of life, but that neither the causes nor the 'cures' of such damage can usefully be treated as 'internal' matters. I would not claim that we do not at times conduct ourselves 'pathologically', but I do claim that we are all, at the outset, innocent victims of *social* pathology rather than harbourers of some kind of psychological abnormality.

Though unorthodox, the position I am taking here is, of course, not new: psychology and psychiatry have always had their critics, many of whom have emphasized the role of society in the generation of distress. Nor am I by any means the first to see the need to defend the individual against the incipient moralism of so-called 'psychotherapeutic' approaches, which, however subtly, manage to 'blame the victim'.

Former critiques seem to me to have fallen short, however, in three main respects. First, they have tended (entirely understandably in view of their starting point) not to draw the radical conclusion from their own arguments. From Alfred Adler to R. D. Laing, the voices raised in criticism of individualistic approaches have themselves spoken from an essentially psychotherapeutic standpoint, and if they have seen the causes of distress as social, have shied away from acknowledging *fully* what this must mean for a therapeutic practice which still, for the most part, 'treats' individuals. Second, the theoretical elements of the accounts given by such critics tend similarly to be rooted in the perspective of one kind or another of individual psychology; indeed, most have their origin in Freudian psychoanalysis. Third, the vision of society offered concentrates most heavily on the person's immediate context – usually that of the family – so that the link between wider social influence and immediate personal experience is left obscure. It is largely concern with these three issues which provides the framework for my present undertaking.

In this, as in my previous books, *Illusion and Reality* and *Taking Care*, I have emphasized the limitations of 'psychotherapy' as an 'answer' to emotional distress, and indeed question 'psychology' itself as an undertaking of any real relevance to issues which seem to me essentially political in nature. However, more than in those books, I have here attempted (largely in Chapter Five) to place psychotherapy and counselling in a context which shows their positive (if modest) contribution as well as their limitations. I do not wish to be seen as rejecting therapy and counselling out of hand, though I do think one needs to be mindful of their intellectual blinkers as well as relentlessly critical of the grandiosity of their claims.

Working for three decades as a clinical psychologist in the National Health Service builds a viewpoint rather different from that of many other critics of the psychotherapeutic and psychiatric orthodoxy. My own view is that, more than just a relative difference in perspective, it is actually an advantage to have gained one's experience in the setting of public health rather than private practice, and in a profession (clinical psychology) which is, unlike medicine, relatively free of the responsibilities as well as the abuses of power. It is easier, I believe, to get at the 'truth' concerning people's difficulties if one wields over them not even a possibility of the kind of coercive power available to, for example, psychiatrists and social workers. Contact with 'ordinary people', furthermore, gives one a particularly clear sight of what it is and is not possible to achieve in struggling with adversity; that is to say, the difficulties and distress of people who are not especially privileged and well resourced throw into sharp relief the poverty of conceptions such as 'insight' and 'responsibility'.

The attempt to sketch out a theory of societal influence which forms the core of this book is the fruit of my experience as a clinical psychologist. I have become less and less able to see the people who consult me as having anything 'wrong' with them, and more and more aware of the constraints which are placed on their ability to escape the distress they experience. I have long been aware that their suffering can in no helpful sense be regarded as their 'fault', but it is only relatively recently that I have been able to establish for myself a theoretical perspective which actually seems to make sense of how the individual experience of distress is related to the operation of social influences at the very margins of our awareness. Over the last few years it has increasingly seemed to me that talking about, and refining aspects of, this theory with the people whose experience has helped to form it is, in fact, often found illuminating by them, even though it doesn't end their troubles. It is this which made the book seem worth writing.

What has, perhaps, made the elaboration of this theoretical framework possible more than anything else has been the social, political and cultural events of the last ten years or so. What in the mid-seventies may have seemed to some a relatively unusual, perhaps rather provocative claim – that the causes of our psychological ills lie in our society – seems to me now barely controvertible. The experience of people who suffered from the 1980s, placed in the context of a radical critique of 'therapy', seems to me to open up possibilities for an understanding of distress which has never been clearer. By taking a decade as a 'case study' (Chapter Four) I hope that I may be able to set up sufficient resonance with readers' experiences to make the rather more abstract theoretical account of Chapter Three come to life, as well as to illustrate the 'inside out' nature of my whole project.

I have written the book very much with the general reader in mind. Trying to write a book which neither assumes specialist knowledge nor panders to some – very likely imaginary – conception of popular taste does, however, present its difficulties, and to the extent that there may indeed be two stools, one runs a risk of falling between them.

A century of academic and professional involvement in psychology and psychotherapy has trained generations of researchers and practitioners to expect their intellectual fare to be delivered in certain kinds of package and certain kinds of style. The packaging is reflected in the way bookshop shelves have become compartmentalized into specialist areas – 'psychology', for instance, is usually split into myriad subsections which must surely be mystifying to anyone not trained to find his or her way around (it's bad enough for those who are). The style of presentation is probably also something which deters the general reader: all those footnotes and unexplained references to 'evidence', which is taken for granted as within the reader's reach.

The layperson, on the other hand, seems often to be expected not to want to be taxed by his or her reading matter. Complex issues and doubtful theories may thus be presented confidently and declaratively, rather in the 'psychologists have shown' style; notions are presented as facts, and the reader is in general expected to *receive* rather than to *enter into* the text.

My experience of talking to clients of the NHS about their, often profound, personal and emotional difficulties has convinced me that 'ordinary people' are perfectly capable of expressing and understanding any theory about their problems you care to name. They are not particularly reassured by simplistic answers, they are not impressed by pomposity, and can detect intellectual and professional bullshit a mile off. On the other hand, of course, they are often not in possession of the educational equipment necessary for deciphering the formal theories and methods underlying the procedures they are subjected to, or for an elegant exposition of their own insights.

There is, of course, a big difference between talking to people and writing for them, and I cannot pretend that this book will prove effortlessly comprehensible to everyone. It is not, I hope, a simplistic book and it may at times make demands on the reader's intellectual resources, but it does not assume possession of resources beyond those available widely to anyone who reads and thinks.

Trying to elucidate for a general readership the nature of distress and the context in which it occurs has, in contrast to beavering away within the narrow sphere created by the academic/ professional division of labour, some interesting consequences. It makes one question one's assumptions and clarify and sharpen the principles and practices which have become the unquestioned routine of one's day-to-day work. All the familiar, dust-laden clutter of received ideas has to be dragged out from the murk of the ivory tower and submitted to a critical scrutiny which takes very little for granted. Conceptual issues have to be clarified and made comprehensible to a commonsense intelligence and their relations with each other made intelligible; practices have to be explained and justified.

So far as the present work is concerned I have found myself having on the one hand to spell out a quite detailed theory of societal influence while on the other to tackle philosophical and ethical issues which rarely seem to make much of an appearance outside a very small and rather claustrophobic academic world. It is one of the sorrier consequences of the compartmentalizing induced by a 'market' in intellectual activity that theorizing should become the exclusive province of specialists in universities (social scientists and philosophers) capable for the most part of being understood only by each other.

One cannot in my view consider the issues with which this book deals without a carefully formulated framework in which to make observations and a speculative appraisal of the meaning of what one observes. To this extent both theory and philosophy are highly relevant to the everyday lives of all of us, and if I risk the scorn of academics for trampling on their grass, I make no apology: it's high time that we tried to break down the cultural barriers between those who make a business of thought and those who are not aware that they are thinking. I say this not out of any Philistine contempt for intellectuals, but because of my awareness through talking to 'ordinary people' in distress of how relevant to their difficulties intellectual considerations are, and how capable they are of making good use of them.

One cannot, then, hope to understand the nature of emotional distress without facing some of the philosophical issues which have always preoccupied people who speculate about what it is to be, and to suffer as, a human being. There can be little doubt that we all do think about these issues in one form or another, but few people encounter 'philosophy' in its formal, academic aspect, and if they do are unlikely to find its rarefied atmosphere one which they can tolerate for long. It is with some hesitation that I have (particularly in Chapter Six) introduced themes in this book – for example, concerning 'truth', 'ethics', 'free will', etc. – which are the staple diet of academic philosophy, mainly because I am aware that to do so will seem to the professionals absurdly ambitious. However, these *are* issues which cannot be evaded when we come to think about the causes of our ills, and if 'ordinary people' are to expand their understanding of them beyond self-blame and pop psychology, they are going to have to get to grips with philosophy too.

I have tried as far as possible to avoid making the text too didactic and academic. I must confess that this has not been difficult. I feel much happier with ideas, conceptions, ways of understanding as organic, changing things to be used in the living of life, rather than as intellectual property which has to be registered, pored over and obsessively criticized. I have always found reading books less like compiling mental catalogues than like eating meals. Some are indigestible and quickly excreted, others (the best) are enormously nourishing and enjoyable, but the details hard, after a time, to hold on to. Like food, ideas become part of one's physical make-up; they are essential to one's continued existence, but one cannot necessarily remember where and when one acquired them.

I would much prefer this book itself to be regarded as a reasonably nutritious meal than as, for example, a potential text for A level psychology. In the interests of readability, I have in any case not peppered the text with as many references as I could have done, and have kept footnotes to a minimum. Many people, past and present, have contributed to the ideas in the book, and where I am aware of their contribution I have acknowledged it in the text. There may be others whose thought has been so well digested that I can no longer distinguish it from my own; if any of them are living, I hope they will take this as a compliment rather than an act of plagiarism.

I hope this approach to documenting the provenance of the arguments to be set out in the following pages will not be regarded as too cavalier. It may perhaps lead to a suspicion that those arguments are of doubtful intellectual parentage. However, I would claim that, though they cannot be identified with any particular 'school', they are not without a pedigree. 'Schools' in psychology, and in particular what I shall call 'brand name' approaches to psychotherapy and counselling, have always seemed to me too cosily like clubs which offer the reassurance of association with 'people like us' rather than being forums for intellectual liberation and discovery. The idea that a particular group of professional experts could corner the market in 'psychology' seems patently absurd. On the other hand, one cannot but be part of a tradition, and I would be far from wanting to disown the influences which have shaped my approach.

I would, for example, be more than happy to be associated with those critics of orthodox psychiatry and psychology who have striven to place the burden of responsibility for distress on the social context rather than the individual (their names will occur throughout the text). More broadly, I think there may be a lot to be said for trying to refract some of the inspired ideas of European (in particular French and German) thinkers through the kind of commonsensical prism one tends to acquire from British empiricism; my understanding (which I freely acknowledge may well not be theirs) of both Michel Foucault and Jürgen Habermas has, for example, contributed greatly to what follows. More broadly still, I wonder how possible it is to escape from one's intellectual and cultural origins even if one wanted to: though, as David Jenkins points out,[1] Christendom no longer rules European culture, it is virtually impossible not to be bound by Christian ethics.

I offer no simple answers in this book. Though this seems to irritate some people, who, so far as I can see, tend to equate a lack of answers with 'pessimism' or even 'depression', it seems to me only sensible. If there were any simple answers to the kinds of problems I shall try to elucidate, they would surely have been found long ago. There has certainly been no shortage of suggestions, and it is precisely the fact that these suggestions have signally not worked that leads one to try again to clarify the nature of the difficulty. To proffer solutions for problems we are barely beginning to understand does nobody any service. This, in fact, is something about which nearly all clients of psychotherapy would agree: being told 'the answer' to your predicament (the most frequent strategy of well-meaning friends and relatives) is usually experienced as profoundly unhelpful, and is exactly what drives people to seek professional help.

Before we can even think about what an appropriate 'answer' might look like, we need to penetrate the ideological obscurity which surrounds the whole question of emotional distress. Success in this latter project, though, might have some interesting effects. It would probably not reduce to any perceptible degree the psychological pain endemic in our world, but it might help to

1. See David Jenkins, Bishop of Durham, & Rebecca Jenkins, *Free to Believe*, BBC Books, 1991.

lift from people the curse of 'abnormality', so that they could at least live their lives as themselves, and understand their own experience as valid.

It is precisely the *validity* of people's experience that I have tried to demonstrate by the use of 'case material' in the following chapters. Above everything, it seems to me, the judgemental clinical eye of psychology and psychiatry needs to be replaced by a respectful appreciation of character, i.e., of the manifold, resourceful, ingenious and, most often, courageous ways in which people of all kinds and conditions come to engage with their fate. I have done my best to give an accurate impression of how the material influences of the social environment ultimately impinge upon and are received by a range of characters who are modelled upon people I have encountered in my work. For obvious reasons I have fictionalized these characters, and not one of them could be identified as anyone personally known to me, though all of them are, I hope, widely recognizable as sharing predicaments typically affecting many people, including, of course, many of those likely to read this book.

CHAPTER ONE

Psychology and Distress – The Story So Far

So far as psychology is concerned, business is booming as never before. What used to be the esoteric preserve of a minor branch of the Academy and a handful of slightly eccentric doctors is now a growth industry whose principal products – counselling, psychotherapy, psychometric testing, etc. – are familiar to everyone. One can't travel far through life before encountering some aspect of psychological thinking or practice. If not before birth, through concerned parents' perusal of the child rearing manuals, then soon afterwards as the infantile object of postnatal care. And if not then, the older child will certainly not escape the influence of 'developmental' and educational psychology once he or she starts school. In later life, psychology comes at you from every direction: from magazine questionnaires on your love life to personality tests which decide whether or not you get a job.

The concern of this book is with the experience of psychological and emotional distress, and here, of course, psychology is in its element. Apart from psychoanalysis, which formed the exclusive practice of a tightly regulated, largely medical club, fifty years ago psychology's involvement in the treatment of 'mental disorder' was virtually nil. In the years following the Second World War, however, the scene was transformed, and a field which had been considered more or less the sole province of medical psychiatry is today wide open for pretty well anyone with a plausible psychological idea to stake his or her claim to putting it into practice. Nor are the theories and techniques of psychologists who succeeded in storming the fortress of psychiatry contained within the strictly 'clinical' sphere: they spill out into the domestic and working world of 'ordinary people', who are as likely to encounter programmes of 'stress management' at work as they are 'relationship counselling' at home.

Some benefits no doubt stem from this transformation. Not so long ago people struggling with emotional pain and distress had little choice but to give themselves over to the mysteries of medical treatments, which they were not permitted to question, but which as often as not left them drugged or electrically stunned into bemused conformity with what they took to be the laws of science. Now, a whole range of 'treatments' and procedures exists, which offers comprehensible accounts of psychological problems, the fundamentals of which can be learned at evening classes. People can now take an active interest in their own psychology – indeed they can hardly avoid doing so – and even if the official channels of help still leave a lot to be desired, the labyrinths of professional mystique are not as impenetrable as they were.

Psychiatry, to be sure, still holds sway in the field of emotional distress, and seeks with habitual arrogance to define what may and may not count as 'mental illness' and what are its appropriate treatments, but its grip is loosening. Apart from the 'psychodynamic' therapies which derive from the psychoanalytic school, there are many other kinds of therapy for the sufferer to choose from: 'behavioural' approaches, 'cognitive' approaches, Client-Centred Therapy, Transactional Analysis, Gestalt Therapy, Rational-Emotive Therapy, and hundreds of other varieties of therapy and counselling, which are flourishing in a rapidly deregulating market.

As the result of all this we may, perhaps, have developed a rather more tolerant and flexible understanding of our personal and emotional difficulties; they may be less tinged with incomprehension and dread than they were when murky conceptions of 'madness' and 'mental breakdown' formed the limits of most people's knowledge. People who can talk about the 'stress' affecting them may be less estranged from themselves than those who could view their psychological interior only as a dark and well-kept medical secret. But what does the psychological boom really indicate? Is it a response to increasing pressures within society? Is it the fruit of a developing scientific understanding of distress? Do we really know ourselves better, and are we curing our psychological ills more successfully than before?

It is interesting that there are, in fact, no satisfactory answers to these questions. There is certainly no evidence that the wider availability of psychological theories and techniques is leading to a decrease in psychological distress, and the burgeoning of such approaches is not founded on any scientifically established evidence of their validity and effectiveness. Nor is there any indication that the relative 'user-friendliness' of psychological approaches leads to people's being able to understand themselves any better than they ever have. We are looking, I would suggest, not so much at a breakthrough in enlightened understanding of distress as at the success of an enterprise.

Psychology, you would think, is a pretty serious and pretty complicated undertaking. Given the importance of its aims and implications, the complexity of its subject matter, and the moral and philosophical intricacies involved in the study of a species by itself, one might expect to find on entering its territory an intellectual structure at least as complex and imposing as nuclear physics (certainly such seems to have been the expectation of some of its earlier explorers like Freud and Jung). What one does encounter, however, is more like a bazaar.

There are, it is true, pockets in academic psychology where painstaking observational work is undertaken and ingenious experiments performed. However, in that aspect of psychology most likely to touch the lives of the 'ordinary person' – psychology as applied to emotional distress – there is less a unified discipline than a motley of competing factions, each trying to demarcate its own domain, patent its own procedures, and prevent intruders from entering its territory.

The pattern was set by psychoanalysis, which at times in its history looked more like a secret society than an intellectual or scientific undertaking (Freud's distribution of rings to the inner circle of his chosen disciples provides an indication). In fact, psychoanalysis developed from being an exclusive club into a cross-national business which sought and seeks to restrict its practice to initiates, and only in the most distant respects could be said to resemble a branch of knowledge. I do not want to suggest that there is anything particularly disgraceful or necessarily even undesirable about this, but only that it runs completely counter to academic tradition, and marks therapeutic psychology out from nearly all other forms of scientific pursuit in a way which must cast doubt on any claim practitioners make to scientificity. One wonders how physics might have progressed had Newtonians refused to truck with Einsteinians, and so on.

In this way, psychoanalysis became the first in a line of 'brand name therapies' all of which to a greater or lesser extent took exclusivity as a criterion of their validity. Gestalt Therapy, Transactional Analysis, Rational-Emotive Therapy, and many others, all emphasize the distinctiveness of their beliefs and procedures, institute training courses with restricted entry, and accredit recognized practitioners; they all but register their trademarks.

In most cases the theory and practice of brand name therapies are far from being the patiently accumulated knowledge of an industrious academic community, but represent rather the hastily elaborated ideas of one more or less charismatic figure who developed personal therapeutic style into a pseudotechnical blueprint for all (who join the club) to follow. In every case we need only look at the basic theoretical constructs to read off the particular preoccupations of the leader. Psychoanalysis reflects Freud's somewhat mechanistic concern with the gloomy engine-room of psychic deviance; Analytical Psychology speaks to Jung's fascination with religion and the more esoteric aspects of cultural anthropology; Carl Rogers builds Client-Centred Therapy in response to his belief in the self-creativity and fundamental benignity of human nature, while conviction in the power of positive thinking guides Albert Ellis to Rational-Emotive Therapy.

It does not seem to occur to the researchers who sedulously compare and contrast such approaches in the hope of establishing scientifically which is 'right' that, representing as they do the whole range of human resourcefulness in confronting personal pain, they are all equally right and equally wrong. So far as Freud, or Jung, or Rogers developed some useful ideas about how to make sense of life, they may help you make sense of yours, and if you wish to consult one of their followers, you would be wise to enter the booth which seems most congenial to you.

For what are on offer in the psychotherapeutic bazaar are not so much – indeed, are not at all – substantiated theories of psychological damage or demonstrably effective cures of emotional pain and confusion, but a range of more or less homespun philosophies of life and the attendant strategies they spawn for trying to cope with it. Just about every conceivable formula is on display, ranging from the entirely biological (distress is a question of nerves, synapses and body chemistry, its cure a matter of appropriate physical readjustment) to the entirely spiritual (psychological equilibrium depends upon the balancing of various kinds of purely internal mental forces). The majority consist of a plausible mixture of outside influences and the internal processing of them – for example, of traumatic events and their subsequent therapeutic reappraisal – such that few people are likely seriously to baulk at submitting themselves to their ministrations.

There was a time when 'scientific' doubts about the efficacy of psychotherapy, broadly conceived, placed something of a brake on its acceptance, certainly within official medical spheres, but also to an extent within the wider culture. That barrier has now collapsed, and it occurs to hardly anyone to question the desirability of therapy and counselling at times of distress – indeed, the therapy industry has succeeded in gathering round itself an aura almost of moral piety: to call the efficacy of 'counselling' into question comes close to committing a kind of solecism.

In view of the absence of clear and convincing evidence for the efficacy of *any* approach to psychological 'treatment', this state of affairs requires an explanation. In essence, I think the explanation is quite simple: 'psychology' in this area flourishes so spectacularly a) because we so *want* it to be effective, and b) because it's impossible to demonstrate that it *isn't* effective.

It is not really possible to elaborate these two points satisfactorily without anticipating too fully arguments to be spelt out in the rest of this book, but perhaps I may at this point sketch what I mean in broad outline.

THE DESIRE FOR EFFECTIVENESS

Despite there being an extremely wide range of theoretical ideas and practical procedures, many of them markedly incompatible with each other, there are nevertheless some general features which almost all approaches to therapy and counselling have in common. The most obvious of these is that the explanation and treatment of psychological distress are negotiated through the social transactions of two people: the 'patient' and the 'therapist'. It seems almost so self-evident as to be beyond question that if you are suffering for reasons you can't immediately understand and rectify, you are best advised to consult an expert who will be able both to explain your difficulties and to offer an appropriate remedy for them. If in trouble, it seems indisputable that one's only recourse is to someone who can help, and if relatives and friends have been, as they so often are, unable even after their best efforts significantly to ease your pain, then a *person* must be sought who possesses the necessary knowledge and expertise to do the trick; there is scarcely any other way one could conceive of the trick being done. It is this paradigm of help – deliverance through a personal relationship – that underlies and legitimates the role of the counsellor, the priest, the physician, sorcerer and astrologer.

Very often the need for solidarity with a person who is *perceived* as possessing power in relation to the individual's predicament outweighs any rational assessment of how effective that power actually is. Magic flourishes at the turn of the twentieth century no less vigorously than it did during the seventeenth. People still consult healers and astrologers, fortune-tellers and spiritualists in the confident belief that they possess effective powers of explanation and cure, and medicine itself is replete with procedures and practices for which there is no scientifically demonstrable justification. There is a great deal of comfort to be gained from association with someone who is able to convince you that s/he knows what s/he is doing, even if s/he doesn't.

The phenomenon of comfort is one which I shall explore in some detail in Chapter Five, but for the present I wish merely to register that it is more than anything the comfort derived from associating with an 'expert' perceived as powerful which sustains the practice of 'therapy' from the point of view of the 'patient' or 'client'.

It is important to recognize both the strengths and the weaknesses implicit in this state of affairs. 'Comfort' is certainly not a spurious or somehow invalid phenomenon. If you are comforted by the optimistic vision of your fortune-teller (and it would be a foolish fortune-teller who was not optimistic), there is no reason to denigrate fortune-telling simply on the grounds of its lack of scientificity. Lots of things can be comforting without being scientific – love, for instance. On the other hand, if, as 'experts' often do, your expert claims to have special insights into the nature of reality, and material powers deriving from those insights, then the *grounds* upon which your comfort is derived may well be bogus, and you may find yourself having been seriously misled in your anticipation of future events, etc. Though comfort may be what you get, comfort may not have been what you were looking for so much as some kind of change in your relations with the world.

It is not at all difficult to see why counsellors and therapists should want to conceive of therapeutic theory and practice in the way they do: it is simply in their interest to do so. Far from being an accusation of duplicity or lack of integrity, this is no more than a statement of the obvious, but it is an important one. When considering why we do things, we often tend to leave interest out of account, as if there was something shameful about it. We like to feel, perhaps, that a therapist or counsellor should be animated by nothing other than a desire to help and an absolute confidence in the purity of the knowledge vouchsafed to the profession. But therapists and counsellors need to make a living in the same way as everyone else, and cannot be expected to be attracted to interpretations of their work which call its validity into question in any fundamental way.

Freud's modification of the view that sexual seduction during childhood was the most significant cause of neurotic disorder in later life, into one which saw such seduction as no more than the child's wishful fantasy, need not be understood so much as a moral failure on Freud's part (which is how Jeffrey Masson interprets it[1]) as an example of the way in which interest works upon us all. Hypocrisy gets in the way of clear understanding: none of us is free from the pressures which lead us to justify our practices in accordance with our enterprise, and 'truth' cannot be totally detached from interest. Psychotherapists cannot be blamed for believing that the help they offer is effective in the way they commonly conceive it to be (i.e., as more than 'mere' comfort), but at the same time their claims may not be objectively valid.

The person in pain must have someone to turn to – for a socialized being no other recourse seems reasonably possible. And the space which that person's need creates is very likely to be filled by a therapist or counsellor whose sincere belief in therapeutic efficacy is coupled with his or her own personal need

1. Jeffrey Masson, *The Assault on Truth: Freud's Suppression of the Seduction Theory*, Fontana, 1985.

to survive in the world. These two factors alone would be enough to guarantee a place for 'psychotherapy' in modern society. But there is a third, very powerful factor which may well be mainly responsible for having given 'therapy' the impetus to thrive as robustly as it has.

This is what one might call the societal influence: i.e., the interest of a social system in there becoming established a view of and approach to psychological pain which conceives of it as a problem caused and cured *within the immediate ambit of people's personal lives*. Since it is this influence which I shall attempt to describe and to challenge in the rest of this book, I shall not say very much more about it at this point, but it is important to note both how pervasive and how rationally unsupported the view of emotional pain as individual 'psychopathology' has been.

The notion that there is something 'wrong' with the person in distress which has to be put 'right' is absolutely central to the medical and psychological disciplines which have grown up over the past 150 years. For this to become the received view, distress had, of course, to be defined as 'pathology' or 'abnormality', so that the focus on painful human experience became narrowed down to the single individual and what had gone wrong either biologically inside the body or 'psychologically' in some kind of nonmaterial (and essentially mysterious) interior space.

An immense amount of effort and ingenuity has gone into identifying, categorizing, isolating and treating these physical and mental faults; they have constituted the *raison d'être* of entire professions; they have received enormous attention from social planners and political policy makers; they have consumed vast sums of public and private money. And yet the evidence that despair, confusion, misery and madness can really usefully be conceived of as varieties of 'pathology' is slender in the extreme, and, even at its most persuasive, rests on the ideological interpretation of otherwise ambiguous research findings rather than on any intellectually compelling demonstration of its validity. (Medically trained psychiatrists, for example, are likely to assert that 'schizophrenia' is indisputably a form of 'mental illness', while many nonmedically trained psychologists will point to the lack of any consistent evidence for this view.[2])

A society which, even if inadvertently, creates distress in its members is highly likely to develop institutional systems for distracting attention from the more unfortunate consequences of its organization and absorbing their worst effects. It seems obvious that preventing the level of critical analysis from extending beyond the individual to the nature of the society itself would be greatly to its advantage. In circumstances such as these, rational evidence is likely to be the last thing anyone takes any notice of.

THE IMPOSSIBILITY OF DEMONSTRATING EFFECTIVENESS

The second factor I identified above as contributing to the robust survival of counselling and therapy despite the general lack of evidence for their efficacy was the fact that it is impossible to demonstrate that they are not efficacious.

There are undoubtedly very many people whose personal experience of psychiatric and psychological treatments – as recipients as much as practitioners – would lead them indignantly to reject what they are likely to take as my implication that such treatments do not 'work'. The problem, however, is that one is not in this area dealing with procedures which have a precise – or even an imprecise – criterion of success or failure. Psychotherapists and counsellors cannot even agree on what they are *trying* to achieve, let alone on whether or not they have achieved it.

Whatever criterion of psychotherapeutic success one takes, the question can always be posed as to whether or not there would not be more appropriate criteria. Do people have to *feel* better after a course of treatment, or do they have to *behave* differently?

2. In this latter regard, see Mary Boyle, *Schizophrenia: A Scientific Delusion?*, Routledge, 1990.

If they *say* they feel better, do they have to demonstrate in the actual conduct of their lives that they *are* better? Do those close to them have to agree that they're better; what if people *say* they're better and their families say they're worse? Does being 'better' have to show up biologically in some way, for example in the measurement of physiological indications of 'stress'; how might one interpret a situation where subjective satisfaction in fact goes with high levels of stress? What is a 'mentally healthy' way of life – for instance, is compliance better than opposition, or assertiveness preferable to meekness?

Such questions can be multiplied endlessly, and though they are ceaselessly addressed by workers in the field of outcome research in the psychological therapies, they are never resolved. Their lack of resolution seems to be taken by most as a tiresome indication of the complexity of the issues, or the lack of adequately sensitive and sophisticated statistical methods of data analysis, and so on, but what seems not often to be squarely faced is that they *cannot* be resolved.

For the problem psychologists and psychotherapists are addressing is not really a technical one of how to cure an illness or adjust an abnormality, but how to live a life, and that is simply not a closed question of the kind which can expect a simple answer. For example, whether *feeling* better is or isn't preferable to *behaving* better is not a technical, but an ethical issue, and there is no court – scientific or otherwise – in which it can be professionally decided. It is therefore possible to go on practising *any* kind of treatment, since *any* kind of outcome will be *arguably* 'right' (and, of course, equally arguably 'wrong'). Unless 'therapy' or 'treatment' has absolutely no outcome at all, which it would surely be absurd to maintain, it is likely that in a preponderance of cases (those in which no obvious damage has been done) it will be perfectly possible to point to effects which are arguably beneficial.

If psychologists, therapists and counsellors were simply offering their services on the basis that they constituted an interesting experience, there would really be no problem about all this, but of course they are not: they are, usually explicitly, offering a professional-technical service which lays claim to demonstrable effectiveness. Their difficulty is not that such claims have, to date, not been supported, but that they couldn't be, because there are no criteria for the satisfactory living of life.

It is worth noting that this is not the predicament of professional workers in disciplines which might be seen as not all that dissimilar, in some ways at least, from psychology. Teachers, for example, can be held to account according to specifiable criteria of what constitutes learning: either pupils have acquired the knowledge and abilities the teacher purports to teach, or they have not. More like astrology, however, psychology is able to maintain its credibility on the grounds of the plausibility or impressiveness of its procedures rather than on the achievement of concrete results (this is a point which emerges compellingly from Keith Thomas's *Religion and the Decline of Magic*).

What is suggested by the foregoing is that the success of the psychological professions is achieved through the *performance of functions* which have little to do with the explicit rationale offered by the professions for their activities. They have not, in fact, constructed a scientifically established account of psychological 'disorder' from which may be deduced effective procedures of 'treatment'. They have, on the other hand, developed a luxuriant set of conceptions and practices which: a) provide people with more or less plausible perspectives on their difficulties and dispense comfort to them while they try to grapple with their predicament; b) constitute a flourishing business for an army of practitioners; c) establish intellectual and professional legitimacy for the view that emotional distress and confusion are in essence personal matters of individual development and relationship and hence are not seriously to be laid at the door of 'society'.

To a worldly eye there is nothing in this to get terribly outraged or upset about: it merely suggests that, like any other human undertaking, psychology is not all it appears to be, that its motives are mixed and its practitioners not always fully aware of, and able to make explicit, the nature of their enterprise.

There is, however, a serious casualty of this state of affairs, and that is the rational understanding of distress. Emerging from the labours of thousands of academic and professional psychologists, psychiatrists and others, there is, after over a century, practically nothing in the way of a clear account of what gives rise to the kinds of difficulties which drive people to consult the experts, nor is there any agreement on what might reasonably be expected to lead to their reduction. There seems little possibility of the 'brand name therapies' coalescing into anything remotely like a workable theory of distress, or of substituting the incoherent breadth of competing approaches with a deeper consensus on the nature and genesis of our ills.

It would take an optimist of outstanding proportions to expect a mere book to make any difference to this state of affairs, but nevertheless I think some of the main reasons for it are discernible, and need to be stated at every opportunity. The principal of these is that psychology has consistently overlooked the most essential ingredient of distress: the ways in which *power* is exercised over people. It is with exploring the significance of this omission that much of the rest of this book will be concerned.

CHAPTER TWO

'When I Was Little' –
The Experience of Power[1]

It is indeed surprising how little psychologists have had to say about power. You might think, after all, that a discipline which concerned itself with motivation, which set itself the task of discovering the mechanisms which set people ticking, would be quick to observe the kinds of organized and directed pressures which bear down upon us and shape our activity through the application of various degrees of force – coercion at one extreme, incentive or persuasion at the other. But power is rarely mentioned – indeed, it seems in general to attract a kind of fastidious reticence which prevents its becoming explicit in our everyday relations with each other. It is simply not decent to refer to the power manoeuvres which attend our social intercourse.

'Decency' might almost be defined as the ability to shroud the nakedness of our interest. There is, it seems, something very necessary about the typical pretence of the diplomat – the naked pursuit of power is inadmissible, and we repress it. A test of what is decent is no doubt whether or not it is mentionable in polite society. These days it is often more indecent to refer openly to our fundamental appetites for control and domination than it is to our sexual appetite. Sex, certainly, can be discussed without qualms at dinner parties, even down to the revelation of quite intimate personal experience, but openly to impute to an

1. A shorter version of this chapter was delivered in May 1991 as the Eighth Hartop Lecture, University of Durham, and published as an occasional paper by the Durham University School of Education.

individual or group an interest in the acquisition of power is to invite the kind of shock, indignation, incredulity or ridicule which is a sure indicator of the functioning of repression.

This is not to say, of course, that consideration and examination of power is repressed everywhere – politics and sociology, for example, are quite explicit about their interest in the workings of power. But maybe this is because such an interest may be presented as *disinterested*: power is considered at one remove from the person considering it, either as, in the case of politics, a collective activity aimed ostensibly at the public good, or as, in the case of sociology, the study of a process more or less detached from its actual operation. Psychology, on the other hand, is concerned with our personal motives and aspirations and our direct relations with each other, and in these spheres the repression of power seems to operate more insistently.

As a rough, and no doubt far from conclusive, test of this impression, I examined a while ago the indexes of all the psychology texts I could find in the local university bookshop. Out of nine texts, only three listed 'power' and *none* listed the principal medium of its application in our society – money. (There is considerable irony in the fact that, at a time in our history when the successful pursuit of money has attained the status practically of a supreme moral injunction, we remain almost totally silent about what this means for our intra- and interpersonal conduct.)

Even though one very occasionally comes across a psychologist tactless enough to expose our interest in money and power (see, for example, Dorothy Rowe's honest and unsentimental account of what life without money can be like in *Wanting Everything*, HarperCollins, 1991) psychology as a whole tends to function a little like diplomacy: its methods and precepts have been established as much as anything to provide a discreet medium *for* the workings of power, which are themselves left unexamined. Psychology's rendering as internal to the individual constructs such as motive and will, desire and insight, its isolation of the person from a social world and its 'therapeutic' emphasis on his or her own responsibility for personal shortcomings, all serve to provide us with a kind of sanitized technology of conduct which turns totally blind eyes to the crushing and rapacious machinations of power which envelop us as soon as we emerge from the womb.

For power is the social element in which we exist. It is almost impossible to think of a human experience which is not shaped by power, does not carry either a positive or negative charge of power. We are thrown at birth into the most highly charged and potentially shocking field of power which it is possible to imagine. At no other point in life is the disparity of the power between the individual (the infant) and the adults (usually parents) around it likely to be so great. Stamped right at the root of our experience is a message of overwhelming significance – that we have to deal with a world which is immeasurably more powerful than ourselves.

If the field of power around us at that point (and, no doubt, for a while afterwards) is, so to speak, *positively* charged, our whole experience may be built upon an essentially uncritical confidence in the ultimate goodness of the world. If, on the other hand (as too often is the case), we receive a negatively charged shock of, for example, near abandonment or bitter isolation, the rest of our lives may be haunted by a latent 'phobic' dread and vulnerability to panic, or perhaps the insatiable drive for security, which feeds on a ruthless pursuit of wealth or a remorseless concern to expose and exploit the weakness of others.

The world forces on us at the earliest point of our experience strategies for dealing with it which I doubt we ever really abandon. It is not that such early experience constitutes some fundamental kind of mistake or error of judgement which will later need 'psychology' for its correction, but that we are, as it were, immediately seized by the shoulders and spun by irresistible forces to take up our stance towards them. This is no mistake, but confrontation with a relentless reality which exacts from us 'decisions' and 'attitudes' which are truly basic. Do we love or hate, fight or flee, trust or fear, confront or dissemble, confide or hide?

Because such 'decisions' and 'attitudes' really are basic, and formed at a time when language is still a mystery to us, they are formed uncritically. We cannot hold them up to ourselves and examine them; they become rather the inarticulate foundations on which we build the rest of our lives and to which we have throughout a passionate and inexpressible commitment. The world announces itself to us as we open our eyes, and what it says we *know* from that day forth.

Some of the most difficult and puzzling features of psychological distress belong to the time before we could talk, and hence lie fallow in our emotional repertoire as *feelings* laden with inexpressible but extremely powerful meaning. Such feelings burst into life whenever the vulnerabilities on which they rest are nudged into activity by suitably structured constellations of events which act, so to speak, as 'reminders'.

For example, I suspect that the 'psychodynamic' view which relates 'panic attacks' to early experiences of abandonment is often very close to the mark. To observe such an attack – either in oneself or others – is to see someone caught up in a literally dreadful experience of 'abandonedness'. The person feels suddenly drained of supporting power – deserted by power – with no ally and no haven, alone in the middle of a completely alien world.

How insightlessly unfortunate that view of 'childcare' which suggested that babies who disturb their parents' peace should be left to 'cry themselves to sleep'. What failure of empathy could see such 'sleep' as anything but exhausted panic and despair, could fail to imagine the agony of a powerless little creature whose world, from its perspective, had quite literally deserted it? And how inevitable that such an experience, especially if repeated a few times, should come to lie in wait as the not inappropriate response to all those occasions in later life when the threat of abandonment is reiterated. Such threats stir into life what the individual *knows* from his or her earliest experiences.

'Confidence' starts out as confidence in those all-powerful others around the infant to protect it and meet its needs. If, through its experience, the infant comes to know that in certain respects no such confidence is justifiable, that there are certain circumstances in which it will be abandoned to its panic, then the vulnerability to panic stays submerged like rocks beneath the sea of its social world for the rest of its life. And that sea is tidal. If things start to go wrong – at work, say, or with a spouse or partner – then as the waters of relatedness ebb, the rocks begin to appear, and as the person begins to feel more and more exposed (often in an 'exposing' place like a brightly lit supermarket under the gaze of hundreds of strangers) panic once again takes over.

We have all been children, and we all know that to be a child is to be at the mercy of adults. For many of us the experience of childhood was almost inseparable from the experience of fear, in relation to some adults at least. In many ways it is extraordinary that we don't take more account of this at least in our psychology and our pedagogy, but then again we always tend to take most for granted experiences which are more or less universal. 'When I was little' are the words with which many of the people who have talked to me about these issues introduce, in the most matter-of-fact and unemotional tones, stories of terroristic oppression by adults which make my blood run cold. I am struck by what a world of meaning lies within those words, despite (or perhaps because of) their being uttered not with any conscious poignancy, but as a kind of unreflective formula, identifying a mere chronological period rather than a state of being.

But state of being it was, being little and being powerless: not only dependent on others for all the material necessities, not only without access to more or less all effective means of power and influence, but also physically at the mercy of those who wielded all this power. The whole of our early experience is acquired in a state of 'littleness' through which most of us come to accept without question – even without noticing it – a world which is shaped and structured through and through by powers we have virtually no alternative but to obey.

'When I was little' is thus frequently the introduction to a tale of (often, of course, unintended) indifference, callousness, exploitation, neglect, tyranny and mystification which leaves the listener speechless with indignation but which is told with a tolerance and unconcern themselves testifying to the mundaneness of it all, the sheer banality and universality of the abuse of the powerless. As adults we would be outraged by treatment which as children we accept – and are expected to accept – without demur. As a child you may be publicly assaulted in ways which would, if you were an adult, undoubtedly lead to the imprisonment of your assailant. We are able to demand respect from children for actions towards them which if they were a few years older would be regarded as criminal.

I am not wanting to suggest that this state of affairs – i.e., the inevitable disparity in power between child and adult – is *necessarily* wrong (though there is no doubt that it is very often abused in the ways I've indicated) but merely that it is so, and that the experience of the child – characterized most centrally in its 'littleness' – imposes a certain kind of orientation towards power. That orientation is largely an uncritical one, its character determined in advance by the terms in which we customarily legitimate relations between the powerful and the powerless. In this way the 'proper' attitude of children towards adults, the little towards the big, is 'respect', and the striking thing as people relate the sometimes horrifying tales of their childhood is the respectful tones in which they do it.

Mrs Johnson, for example, had for fifty years kept to herself the scenes which were enacted between her father and herself from when she was a girl of about six or seven (her mother died when she was five). As she told her story she became tearful and angry for the first time at how, according to an alcoholic whim, he would stand her in front of him as he sat in his fireside chair and roar abuse at her for half an hour or more. He used to yell obscenities at her which she could only just bring herself to repeat, and when she finished talking she was still superstitiously fearful of her long-dead father's revenge for the betrayal. 'I've never told anybody that before,' she said, 'out of loyalty'. 'Loyalty' – the word was mentioned in passing, and is indeed unremarkable enough unless one stops almost deliberately to reflect upon it. For what can exact such loyalty? Only the operation of an utterly unjust and indiscriminate power to which we become enslaved by virtue of not much more than our relative littleness. The child cowers under the demands of such power as under the vengeful eye of a jealous and implacable god.

Such power acts as a stamp on the child's experience, it impresses its content on the growing organism with a force which marks that organism – the person – for ever. Power exacts respect and 'loyalty' towards whatever it presents as its central demand. The stances the child takes up towards the issues life presents it with are shaped and authorized by power. The parental word is the word of God. (Just think, for example, with what feelings of unease you try to disregard even trivial parental nostrums and injunctions which you now know to be nonsense.)

In Mrs Johnson's case, her father's fireside entertainment set the pattern for her relationships with men for life: she had two marriages and a couple of other long-term relationships with men who without exception turned out to be capricious and sadistic in one way or another, and who quite literally abused her as her father had done. She was an extraordinarily perceptive and sensitive woman, highly intelligent, though not well educated, and I had no reason to doubt her when she said she loved the man she was currently with. He was considerably younger than she, sometimes charming, but he regularly taunted and derided and occasionally hit her. She was typically perceptive about him and understood him, and she loved him *because* she understood him (much, no doubt, as she used to – had to – understand her father). She could not love or be interested in a man whose character had not, so to speak, been authorized by her father's example; her whole life was bent towards loving and understanding the agonized, drunken, terrifying man with whom she spent alone so many of her early years.

We often overlook, I think, the close relationship of love to power. We prefer to think of love as unsullied by the indecency of power, or even opposed to it. And yet, when we are little, the form our loving takes is exacted by power. The relatively helpless infant and child can no more choose the characteristics of those he or she is dependent on than can the family dog, and, uncomfortable as it might be to suggest it, our learning to love contains a strong element of choiceless dependence.

There is, of course, unselfish love, but that is not the variety which attaches itself to our desire. The kind of love we crave, and the lack of which drives us to despair, the love which cements our relationships positively or negatively destroys them, the shape, that is, which childhood experience gives to our loving, is always stamped by the impress of power. For the most part (unless, that is, our early experience has been cast in a 'sado-masochistic' form) we are not interested in or moved by the love of the powerless. We neither love nor wish to be loved by people we see as having no power. We may be hypnotized or enslaved by the powers we detect in a lover – echoes, quite probably, of the nameless ingredients of a parent's rule – and enraged and betrayed if they are withdrawn from us, but even the adoration of someone who has no such hold over us is just an embarrassment. The tramp who sits next to you on the park bench may be as wise as Solomon, but you are unlikely to attach to his words the importance you would to those of a complete idiot who happened to be sitting in an expensive office and had letters after his name.

The nature of the power relation between oneself and others is the unreflected-upon determinant of a whole range of feelings and attitudes one may have towards them. Whether you hate or pity, blame or excuse, desire or dismiss is likely to depend on the extent to which you see the other as having a degree of power in relation to you which you may either fear or covet. It is easy to be cool and dispassionate towards those one cares nothing for, i.e., who stand outside the immediate field of power in which one is situated, but as soon as people move into that field they are likely to become the objects of a nervous, prickly appraisal which anxiously scans them for threat and opportunity. It is particularly difficult to see that what we often take to be matters of fact – for example, objective descriptions of people around us – are really distorted rationalizations shot through with defensiveness and soaked in self-interest.

Perhaps the main advantage of the situation of the psychotherapist or counsellor is that it minimizes the operation of certain kinds of power-saturated dependency which make simply understanding another person difficult. Blame can only give way to compassion if an unusually asymmetrical power structure is established between the people concerned. Similarly, 'professional' interest in someone can only replace desire or dislike if the more usual interdependences and mutual demands of social intercourse are deliberately suspended, as they are in situations, like psychoanalysis and the confessional, where only one person talks and the other listens.

But the positive or negative charge of power cannot be separated out from our relationships, therapeutically or otherwise, as by some alchemical centrifuge. We can, of course, attempt consciously to give our relations with others a certain power structure (as in the therapeutic relationship) but we cannot after the event somehow detach experience from the impress of power, and, perhaps through some purported process like 'cognitive restructuring', give it a different shape from that which it originally possessed. For example, I think it unreasonable to expect someone who, like Mrs Johnson, has suffered profoundly under the sway of parental tyranny ever to come to experience that force which gave shape to her whole life as anything other than, literally, dreadful. One can, to be sure, invite her to criticize the exercise of that tyranny, and though this might seem to her at first like inviting the wrath of God, she may come after some time to see it for what it was and begin to feel less uncomfortable about the grief and anger attached to her early experience. But she is not going to be persuaded that the orientation to life that experience impressed upon her is somehow a mistake.

The fallacy of the Freudian concept of 'transference' is precisely that it suggests that the impress of power can, through the psychoanalytic technique of 'interpretation', be centrifuged away from one's experience, leaving one able to exercise a detached judgement concerning constructions of events which are somehow real in comparison with the distortions of a past which one was, until they were 'interpreted', 'transferring' on to them. What is experienced under the impress of power is, on the contrary, only too real, and imparts a certain expertise in the possibilities the world has to offer which one is, in a sense, fated to work out for the rest of one's life. Greek tragedy is far truer to the nature of our experience in this way than is psychoanalysis and much of the therapeutic industry which derives from it.

It is the relative obscurity of the historical origins of people's experience which makes their subsequent difficulties often initially so puzzling. Problems which seem at face value to permit of quite simple solutions – perhaps through the almost minimal application of a bit of 'will power' – may seem almost maddeningly resistant to 'treatment' until one begins to see that they have foundations back at a time when the person was in no position to understand or grasp critically what was happening to him or her. Almost none of our experiences are defined *just* by the present, and, more than naive, it is simply false to assume (as does the idea of 'transference') that knowledge of the dimensions of the present alone is sufficient to spell out a rational account of our conduct.

Eating problems – as anyone who has ever had one will know – are a good case in point. Being too fat or too thin, even if only in your own eyes, is not just a matter of needing to eat less or more and adjusting your diet accordingly. For the ingestion of food has a history which is replete with meanings given it under the impress of power. The bulimic woman who secretly stuffs herself at one moment and sticks her fingers down her throat the next becomes subject to an anguish which has its meaning in shadows of her past far too dark for her understanding to penetrate now, and not amenable at all to commonsense injunctions concerning diet.

Take Susan, for example. She is, as she herself acknowledges, vastly overweight and desperate to lose some. She can see as clearly as anyone the simple dietary logic which guarantees the realization of her aim but she simply is not able to put it into practice. Diets end in binges which can involve the guilty consumption of colossal amounts of food, sometimes for quite extended periods of time. Even the achievement of losing weight doesn't seem to help. Perhaps she slowly but surely loses weight for six months. She's delighted with herself, begins to feel she's really cracked it. Then she binges for a week, puts on nearly two stones, and consequently seethes with remorse and anger at herself. The conceptual equipment she brings to the problem is no different from that of most people, and consists mainly of ideas about will power and control. If she's failed she must try harder. *This* time she's so disgusted with herself that she just knows she's not going to lapse again. But she does.

One thing Susan does notice is that she binges more often when she's lonely and missing the warmth of a close relationship. She usually manages to lose quite a bit of weight if she has a boyfriend, but this is a rare event not least because she is convinced that any man who shows an interest in her must be some sort of pervert.

A plausible version of her early relationship with her mother emerges only slowly because at first it is presented as conventionally idealized. Far from being selfless provider, however, it seems that in fact her mother both rejected and neglected her in early life, having a passion for horse racing which took up all her spare time and money. But she was not a feelingless woman and not without a guilty awareness of her shortcomings as a mother, for which she tried to compensate by rather unexpectedly stuffing her daughter with sweets and chocolate from time to time. It seems unlikely that she could find in herself much love for her daughter, but as adults so often do with children, she managed to convey to her the feeling that she would be able to love her more if only she were a *good* girl. And when love was delivered, it came in the form of chocolate.

So what Susan knows about herself – what had been stamped in before she could even think – is that she is not good enough to be loved, but that a form of love is obtainable through the guilty and inconsistent administration of 'treat' foods. Because historically what was, in fact, an irresistible power over her was presented as an issue of her own choice (to be or not to be a good girl) she now construes the inability to help herself over bingeing as a matter of weak will, and the guilt she feels when she stuffs herself, and the hasty secrecy with which she does it, she no doubt also learned at her mother's hands.

It is hard when contemplating the parental tyranny by which so many people have been, and are, subjugated to avoid a tone of indignation, and many of those who have explored this area in psychology and psychiatry – like, for example, R. D. Laing – have been accused of 'blaming' parents for their children's distress. Such accusations are usually misplaced, the discomforted reaction of people unable to distinguish blame from explanation. In fact, it is perfectly possible to see most writers in this area as correctly identifying parents and families as the instruments of oppression without there being any implication of moral condemnation. While it may well be important for individuals themselves to condemn those at whose hands they have suffered (principally as a way of ceasing to condemn *themselves*) it would be utterly inappropriate for the outside observer, who has, of course, incurred no suffering of any kind, to get hot under the collar about what can clearly enough be seen to have taken place with fateful inevitability.

For the causal chain in the transmission of power does not end with parents; the field of power does not coincide with the boundaries of the family. Of course, from the infant's point of view, it *does*, and in the early days of its existence the infant may have no conception of any field of power wider than that of the mother herself (or, if Melanie Klein is right, even of parts of her body). Someone, however, who stands outside the family boundaries as an observer seeking to understand the processes at work could not possibly *blame* parents for what happens to children because he or she can see that the parents are themselves subject to pressures and influences, not to mention histories, over which they in turn have no control.

On the whole, psychology has concerned itself very little with the field of power which stretches beyond our immediate relations with each other, and this has led to very serious limitations on the explanatory power of the theories it has produced. So far as the psychotherapies are concerned, most deal with the context of the immediate family itself – looking, for example, no further than 'Oedipal' conflicts or sibling rivalries for explanations of patients' troubles – and some even concentrate most heavily on the here-and-now of the relation between patient and therapist. Concentration on such microenvironments as these may have some plausibility in terms of reflecting patients' experience of their world, but it is very little use for understanding how they come to be the way they are.

A few theorists of therapeutic psychology have paid more attention to societal influences: Alfred Adler, Karen Horney, Erich Fromm, H. S. Sullivan and Laing all looked out into the wider world for explanations of what was happening to their patients. And all have remained on the fringes of their discipline – not without an honourable mention, perhaps, but certainly without widespread or established approval and lasting reputation. As is suggested in greater detail elsewhere in this book, the reason why such views, though fashionable in their time, have otherwise suffered relative neglect has less to do with any fundamental inaccuracy (quite the contrary) than with, first, the questions they raise about the efficacy of 'therapy', second, the already mentioned discomfort they arouse in those who confuse explanation with blame, and third, the questions they threaten to raise about the nature of the society we live in.

For one of the services performed by orthodox psychology within what Michel Foucault has called the 'discourse of power' has been to reinforce the tendency already established in human beings to look little further than their noses for the causes of their unhappiness. Although most of us are ready to accept that our distress stems from 'circumstances beyond our control', we usually identify such circumstances as those we can see, and have little interest in pursuing their origins out into the further reaches of the social network. Psychology, in encouraging us to restrict our gaze to the microenvironments which provide the context of our personal experience – the ambit of our physical being – wittingly or unwittingly aids the process whereby the machinery of social injustice is kept out of sight.

In fact, of course, our lives are most powerfully controlled by forces that are completely out of sight. It is in many ways a truism that those things which you 'can do nothing about' are the ones which tend to affect your life most profoundly. Our world is structured, then, by powers at varying degrees of distance from us. Those closest to us – proximal powers – are the most salient, the ones which preoccupy us most, the ones focused on by psychology, the most amenable to our personal intervention, and the weakest. Those furthest from us – distal powers – are the least salient, the ones we tend to spend least time thinking about, the ones focused on by sociology and politics, almost entirely impervious to merely personal influence, and the strongest.

A decision made in a boardroom in New York is likely to have a greater impact on a larger number of lives than anything a mere parent can dream up, and yet, of course, its impact will not be *experienced* as anything like as great by each individual considered separately. Most of us don't even know the origin of decisions which may be shaping our lives radically, or indeed that any such decisions have been made, but a father's drunken rage may be experienced as an event of cataclysmic proportions. It is almost impossible for a single individual to shake off his or her personal perspective sufficiently to see how insignificant are the events of the field of power which is immediately open to experience, and yet to give an adequate explanation of how things come to pass even in that individual's world it must in the end become necessary to take account of the distal powers which operate, so to speak, over his or her horizon. It is not that proximal powers don't have the more immediate, and potentially devastating, *effect* on the person – indeed they must do, since it is only through the operation of proximal power that the person can be affected by *anything* – it is rather that the operation of those powers depends in turn on influences much further afield.

Father's drunken rage does not originate within some kind of moral space located inside Father, one, for example, which he can choose to activate or suppress; Father is not a bundle of open possibilities from which he makes, capriciously or otherwise, a selection (though, of course, it will seem like that to the child at the very edge of whose 'power horizon' he stands). Father's alcoholic rage, in fact, has to be accounted for by the influences which operate upon him: some, no doubt, to do with his personal history and some with the circumstances operating on him over which he may have no control (the fact, for example, that he has just been made redundant).

So unused are we to looking for the causes of our distress in the operation of distal powers that one needs to place particular stress on the necessity as well as on the *empirical* justification for doing so – it does not just depend on some theoretical quirk. The influence of political decisions on our lives is perhaps familiar enough, and, though no doubt some would cavil, the effects of unemployment, poor housing, social deprivation and decay are widely accepted as causes of emotional distress and damage. The more distal the powers, the more universal their influence within a given society, and the more likely we are simply to overlook them. As an outsider it is sometimes possible to detect in people's experience the operation of powers which insiders may not notice. I have, for example, been struck by how the doctrines of the Church in Ireland have a sway over the minds of even dissenting individuals such that the 'symptoms' of psychological disturbance are only fully comprehensible through reference to the power of the Church. Laws governing marriage and the reproductive process, for instance, give a significance to marital consummation which renders the act itself vulnerable to forms of 'pathology' rarely encountered in Britain but which often tend to be thought of by the Irish as essentially 'personal' problems.

Even to begin to get an intellectual hold on 'the discourse of power' it is necessary to see how misleading is the almost irresistible perspective given by our personal experience, the perspective determined by our power horizon. The less power one has, the nearer to oneself as centre is one's power horizon. The small child is pressed right up against its towering parents, and comes to see beyond them only when it starts to go to school. Moreover, the little cannot escape a *passionate* relation to the big who overshadow them. The child's involvement with its parents – its love for them, as perhaps also its hate – is closely correlated with the space they occupy in its field of power (in later life the intensity of this emotional involvement with the parents may be maintained by their material rather than their physical dominance; it's much less easy to feel dispassionate towards rich as opposed to poor parents).

Our analysis of our wellbeing (or the lack of it), and what can be done about it, will, unless we make an almost impossibly conscious effort, depend on the limits of our perspective, and that perspective can often be very misleading. The child thinks its parents have the powers of gods. The tea boy, perhaps also the sales manager, thinks that the managing director has insights into the workings of the wider world completely unachievable by him, and hence imputes to him powers he very probably hasn't got. We frequently offer authority for a view by citing the opinion of someone who stands further from the centre of *our* field of power without realizing that in fact they occupy much the same 'power space' as we; though he may seem a long way from you, the perspective available to your boss is determined by much the same institutional limits as is yours.

As long as a social system operates power against the interests of the majority of its members, it will attempt to keep the machinery of power out of sight – well over the power horizon of the ordinary citizen. Even where we operate with power differentials which in principle at least are open to inspection, we still tend to be curiously unaware of their existence, often reticent about and possibly even incapable of describing them. The typical middle-class person, for example, occupies a world of powers and opportunities much less available to the average working-class person – indeed the difference in their availability is partly definitive of class. The manager is trained for and inducted into a world where (relatively) distal powers are mediated linguistically and procedurally by means largely unavailable to the worker. The former knows structure, form, office, protocol, the means of distal communication and influence. The latter knows objects, tools, people, impulses, the making and breaking of social bonds in the proximal world of immediate influence. The former deals in generalities and abstractions, the latter in specifics and feelings. *Of course* middle-class life may be lacking in warmth and immediacy. It can afford to be.

When Mrs Wright, a highly respectable and socially conscientious woman, finally succumbed to despair at the damp and generally sordid condition of her council house, she ended up abusing the housing manager down the telephone and threatened him with a duffing-up by her two large sons. The world of pithy letter writing and veiled hints about personal access to MPs, public health departments, etc. – the paraphernalia of association with power – was completely beyond her ken, and all she achieved by her phone call was a menacing visit from a council minion who frightened her into continuing to suffer in silence.

Although this is all obvious enough, we are still often blithely unaware of the difficulty one person may have in understanding or communicating with another where there is a significant power differential between them. The relatively more powerful are, for example, fond of attempting to solve the problems of the less powerful by offering them advice. However sincerely and helpfully meant, this usually overlooks the fact that the more powerful (most often middle-class) person moves with unconscious ease in a world which contains procedures, resources and knowledge which it would take the less powerful (usually working-class) person years to acquire – by which time, of course, there would no longer be any need for advice.

One way to break the tendency to give well-meant but unhelpful advice of this 'let them eat cake' kind is to invite its donor to imagine going up a social stratum rather than down and trying to conform with the advice he or she would no doubt receive there on how to conduct him or herself. It is widely accepted, for example, that acquisition of the kind of 'taste' necessary for admission to the loftiest circles is a matter of 'breeding' (i.e., life–long application), and few people who share the social stratum I occupy would know how to 'go on' at an aristocratic house party, however clear or kindly the on-the-spot instruction they might receive. It takes time, just for a start, to learn to ride a horse.

In fact, of course, one rarely finds those higher up the social pyramid anxious to impart the secrets of their distinction to those lower down; they are, that is, no more likely freely to distribute what can be called their ideological power to those less well endowed than they are to give away their money.

A woman interviewed on BBC radio news observed: 'The people higher up don't let us little people know what's going on.' The occasion was the fruition of some planning iniquity which had at a stroke diminished her quality of life and that of thousands of other 'little people' while enriching that of one or two 'big people'. And that, of course, is in every sense the secret

of ideological power: to control the perception little people have
of big people's interests, usually merely by obscuring their view.
The power horizon of ordinary people is set not only by the limits
of their own sphere of operations, but by the ability of the more
powerful to screen their own interests and activities behind veils
of 'disinformation', strategically constructed silence, and manipulation of the machinery of knowledge, enquiry and what counts
as truth. More will be said about these processes in the following
chapter, but it is essential to bear in mind if one is to make any
sense of the experience of power that it is not only brute force
(coercive power) and financial muscle (economic power) which
can be wielded to keep 'little people' in their place – the projects
of the powerful may be obscured ideologically just as discreetly
and effectively as the material signs of their wealth may be hidden
behind hedges and walls.

Therapeutic psychology has been remarkably silent about the
actual experience of relative social insignificance – the awareness
of being among the 'little people'. This latter is, of course,
essentially the experience of class, and while a great deal of
sociological attention has been focused on the class issue, I can
think of no approach within the so-called psychotherapies which
takes seriously the way class position is reflected in the self-
consciousness of the individual. The reason for this, no doubt,
is once again the fact that therapeutic psychology prefers to
overlook difficulties which could not plausibly be dealt with within the confines of the 'therapeutic relationship', and though
individuals are often exhorted by their therapists to 'esteem'
themselves more highly (it is, of course, mainly those in the lower-
class brackets who are going to be disadvantaged by their position),
class is fairly inescapably a social phenomenon, and not one over
which individual people can be expected to exercise a great deal
of control.

For precisely one of the most central features of class occupancy,
looked at from its ideological aspect, is its indelibility. The
ideological preservation of class advantage, as opposed to its

foundation on merely economic power, makes use of indices of distinction which physically mark the person with almost ineradicable signs of superiority or, more important for the understanding of psychological pain, inferiority. Pierre Bourdieu's *Distinction* (Routledge & Kegan Paul, 1984) offers brilliant insights into this process.

Power is maintained within class groupings through the process of distinguishing the superior from the inferior by means of signs which cannot easily be faked. In English society particularly, the possession of money is by no means enough to gain admission to the higher reaches of class distinction. 'Breeding', to pass as genuine, has to show the signs of having been acquired naturally, rather as native speakers of a particular language can usually be distinguished from those who have learned to speak it as a secondary acquisition. What demonstrates the entitlement of the upper classes to their position are the ease and familiarity, the assurance with which they move about a world which is at every level and in every domain peppered with indications as well as tests of their distinction. And it is no accident that the indications of class are so hard to fake – for if they were not, they would, of course, be useless as indications of anything. The aspirated aitch is a good example: if not practised unconsciously from birth, there is nothing more likely to catch out the upper-class impersonator and give him or her away than dropping aitches from where they 'should' be or tacking them on (a particularly telling indication of attempted fraud) where they should not. This is like building a caste mark into the person's brain, a hidden bug in the 'program', which will beep embarrassingly every time he or she tries to slide through the gates of a higher class preserve, which ideologically presents its advantage as birthright.

The lot of the class fugitive, the person who attempts to become free of a disadvantaged background by acquiring the ideological as well as the economic powers of the 'big people', is in many respects an extremely uncomfortable one, and it is perhaps not surprising that it is people in this position who are often possessed by the most virulent snobbery and contempt for the weak and inferior. To venture out of your class and attempt to pass yourself off as an article more refined than it was originally branded is a bit like living undercover in a hostile country, and even the most successful class fugitive is vulnerable to exposure as an impostor by, for example, a buried regional accent suddenly peeping through a treacherous vowel sound. Even if the presentation is near perfect, there are in the background aunts and uncles, cousins and old schoolmates who know a bogus eminence when they see one and may not hesitate to say so. So aspiring social climbers more or less have to turn their backs on their past, fear as well as despise their origins and reject the culture and society to be found there as worthless in every respect. (It is ironic that the impossible vision of a 'classless society' is proffered precisely in the 'yuppie' culture which is so characteristic of the class fugitive. Whatever such a society might actually look like, it would surely not be one in which the insignia of 'lifestyle' are so relentlessly cultivated by the very people who proclaim its classlessness.)

Class disadvantage is a form of injury inflicted on the person at birth. Even those who, in contrast with the class fugitive, heroically stand their ground and fight for social change, who use their experience of oppression to try to modify the system rather than to acquire the secrets of exploitation themselves, even they cannot escape the injurious effects of caste marking. The most admirable working-class leaders often betray a kind of apprehensive awareness of somehow being out of bounds. The uneasy handling by union leaders of the language of the 'educated middle class', so easily lampooned by the unkind satirist, is no doubt an unavoidable consequence of the secondary acquisition (as opposed to the 'inbreeding') of intellectual powers, but the peppering of their speech with expressions such as 'with respect', the bodily posture which is either defiantly stiff or defensively hunched, testify to a fear of the power they challenge which, though certainly not groundless, probably exists less as a response to any immediate reality than as a built-in part of their own experience of themselves as people. The confident slouch of the hands-in-pockets, old Etonian cabinet minister speaks not so much of a current possession of power (on some measures the union boss might possess as much) as of a confidence in social worth which was sucked in with his mother's milk.

People's sense of worth, what one might call their basic self-confidence, stems essentially from two sources: first, their relations as literally little people with the big people who occupied the proximal field of power during infancy and childhood, and second the sense of metaphorical littleness or bigness they later discovered themselves to have been accorded by the more distal powers of a social world which sorts people according to the ideological criteria of class.

The interaction between parental influence and class position often determines the extent as well as the nature of class injury. The latter more easily becomes a permanent disability where the individual's self-regard did not receive its foundation in the loving support and approval of the all-important adults around him or her in childhood. When exposed later to the baleful stare of a remorselessly categorizing and evaluating social world, people who have neither been stamped by positive class distinction nor energetically endorsed, supported and encouraged by parental power find themselves trembling before an exposure from which there is no sanctuary. There is nothing they can call upon 'inside' them – that is, nothing in their history – to place a screen of comfort or protection between themselves and the dismissive judgement of the world; they have no *knowledge* of themselves as worthwhile which they could use to challenge the institutionalized snobbery which keeps them in their place.

The actual experience of people in this position is very rarely accompanied by any awareness of the ideological manipulations of power or illuminated by any critique of the social structure. Their situation is experienced as purely personal, and most would be quite incredulous at explanations of what they feel being couched in terms of social or even historical influences. At the root of their experience is an acceptance of the valuation placed upon them – their worthlessness *is* their personal worthlessness, and they wither before the public gaze as a plant withers before the icy wind. The sense of exposure is indeed central to the experience of someone in this situation: isolated, cut off, surrounded by hostile space, you are suddenly without connections, without stability, with nothing to hold you upright or in place; a dizzying, sickening unreality takes possession of you; you are threatened by a complete loss of identity, a sense of utter fraudulence; you have no right to be here, now, inhabiting this body, dressed in this way; you are a nothing, and 'nothing' is quite literally what you feel you are about to become. The overwhelming reaction to finding yourself in this situation is the need to flee, to find refuge in some 'safe haven' like your home or your car, anywhere protected from the unremitting hostility of public space.

Like so many of those who suffer most from life's unkindnesses, Mrs Lawrence is an intelligent, insightful, gentle and sensitive woman. People respect her and like her, and her husband and children love her, though they and her friends tease her about both her sensitivity and the slightly quirky individuality which the combination of insight and honesty gives to her view of the world. Now in early middle age, she was born and brought up in a notorious urban slum. Her father was a bright, vain man, who spent all he earned on his own clothes and his own comfort – taken mostly in the form of women and drink. He was dissolute rather than brutal, and took absolutely no notice of either of his daughters, though he exploited their cowed and needy mother mercilessly, raging at her contemptuously whenever she complained about her lot, which was often. She gave no support to her daughters, but called upon them to support her, and all her life Mrs Lawrence has had to look after her mother as if mother were in fact daughter.

Mrs Lawrence talks wistfully of the tree-lined avenues where she would like to live, but 'knows' that she has no right to do so – even to wish it is a kind of punishable hubris. An unshakeable knowledge of what she 'is' is carried around with her like a submerged but ever-present grief. She can name the central quality that sums up her nature and her worth, and she is certain that it is patent to anyone who stops long enough to give her the time of day: she is 'rough'. If you dispute this (for 'rough' is about the last description you would apply to this gentle, delicate, emotionally discriminating person), she will smile patiently but a little pityingly at your failure to comprehend.

One of the ideological blocks standing between Mrs Lawrence (and many like her who have shared a similar world) and an enlightening sociopolitical critique of her experience – or the way she interprets it – arises out of a personal acquaintance with social degradation. Despite the romanticizing of life in the old slums by some who seem happy enough not to live in one, people who have, or who live in one of the new slums which have replaced them, have often seen and experienced enough to know that there is a sort of state of ultimate degradation from which even 'roughness' may be positively distinguished, and which, it seems to them, brands its occupants as finally and utterly morally irredeemable. Frequently, the possibility of degradation has a kind of uncanny quality about it which may positively haunt a whole family and turn 'ordinary disasters' (like, for example, a daughter's unintended pregnancy) into nightmarish catastrophes so deeply imbued with shame that recovery seems scarcely possible. It is this state of degradation which tends to get seen by those once traumatized by it as what is meant when people talk of 'poverty', 'working class' or 'socialism'. Any political concern with the environmental damage wrought on those at the bottom of the heap by a social system run by those towards the top tends then to be displaced by an uncompromising moralism about the avoidability through personal effort of apathy, squalor and general moral degeneracy. People raised within sight of ultimate degradation are frequently concerned only to dissociate themselves from it, and have no distal view of the reasons for it; they can speak of the desperation to keep out of it only in the proximal language of personal struggle.

Take, for example, Mrs MacFarlane. She is the second oldest of five children born in a quarter even less favoured than Mrs Lawrence's birthplace. Her two brothers (one actually a half-brother, the result of her mother's indiscretion with a neighbour) were boarded out with grandparents, while she and her two sisters shared the back bedroom of the parental home, she and her older sister sharing a bed. Her mother was an anxious and superstitious woman prone to panicky rages, irrational bouts of over-protectiveness interspersed with a kind of helpless indifference, whose consequently whimsical behaviour was as important to predict as the weather but considerably more difficult. Her father was dispirited, sometimes violent, sometimes warm and kind, often out of work (when he would become depressed and drink a lot). Sometimes, most usually when his wife was pregnant, her father would pay occasional visits to her sister's bed and 'play about' with her, though Mrs MacFarlane maintains that he never involved her in these activities.

Mrs MacFarlane had only the most rudimentary education, not least because her mother singled her out to stay at home and perform those errands which her own attacks of anxiety precluded. However, she expresses herself unusually articulately, reads quite a lot and talks very perceptively about those around her; it comes as a surprise to discover how little formal education she has had.

For almost as long as she can remember she has been running a kind of sexual gauntlet, pursued as a juvenile and adolescent girl by dirty old men and equally dirty young boys as she walked her little brothers along the banks of the local canal; now as a twice-married woman in her mid-thirties she is still (along with most of her female colleagues) regularly cornered in his office by the manager of the cut-price chain store where she works.

Mrs MacFarlane has three children by her first marriage, one of whom has an incurable condition which requires medical equipment not provided by the state and which she cannot afford to buy. Both she and her husband have jobs (hers part time) which together bring in less money than they could get on social security, but her equation of 'poverty' with degradation prevents her from regarding her family as 'poor', and indeed she has, together with her husband, who is a kind and supportive man, fought with all her strength to avoid the kind of degradation she felt so acutely as a child. (One of her least pleasant memories is of how, as a part of her parents' requirement that she should clean the house at weekends, she had to collect up the spent condoms from beneath their bed.)

She is one of those rare people who have a kind of innocent clear-sightedness which rests on a combination of irrepressible honesty and great intelligence. In many ways her intuitive sensitivity is far too finely tuned for the world in which she has found herself, and there is within her a latent conceptual power, an unrequited love of truth that needs desperately to be met by an outside world which understands it. The nearest she has got to finding such a world so far has been the disciplined and morally ferocious irrationality of fundamentalist evangelical Christianity; this has succeeded only in providing her with her first husband (whose violent rages and homosexuality in the end became too much for her) and copious amounts of superstitious guilt about the perfectly natural feelings the sect proscribes but which she is far too honest to deny.

Mrs MacFarlane had not learned to criticize her circumstances; she had simply accepted her proximal reality as the actuality of an unchangeable world, and (with medical encouragement) had interpreted the protests of her nervous system as an indication of weakness and instability rather than as an entirely natural response to painful difficulties. She has the 'naturally' deferential attitude to doctors which hundreds of years of the English class system ineluctably imparts, and her relations with them are reminiscent of the relations she enjoys with God: she is overwhelmed with gratitude for their kindness, utterly demolished by their impatience or ill-concealed contempt, and consumed by superstitious dread whenever her irrepressible perceptiveness sees through the sham of their authority. So she has 'panic attacks' which she douses with tranquillizers. But she certainly doesn't lack the personal resources necessary to gain insight into so-called 'neurotic' defensiveness and to act upon it, and indeed she is a quite unusually courageous person.

In fact, she has come a long way in understanding, controlling and losing much of the fear of her panics, and insight into the real reasons for her frustration and pain gives her glimpses of a possible future which sometimes cause bursts of excited hope. To realize that hope, however, would mean making changes which, added together, are just about insuperably difficult. Just to obtain the level of education she would need to lift herself into a social stratum where she would find answering echoes to her own potentialities would mean her having to turn her back on her past, earn the frightened contempt of her brothers and sisters, threaten her husband's self-esteem almost unbearably for him, and in general enter areas of social, emotional and intellectual unfamiliarity of truly terrifying proportions. And all this quite apart from the prohibitive financial restraints on her becoming able to embark on any kind of programme of self-improvement.

She has already encountered in her own life the essence of Freud's dictum about neurotic misery giving way to common unhappiness but her attempts to act on a growing understanding of her situation have not met with unqualified success. Having been pinned up against his office wall by her sexually harassing manager once too often, she told him where to get off and for a while felt a lot better for it. The end result, however, was a loss of vital overtime and a campaign of more or less subtle victimization if anything less supportable than the unwanted sexual attentions. Despite her obvious intelligence and warm friendliness she failed to get a slightly better job in a marginally up-market chain store largely because her local accent was not considered compatible with the refinement of a saleslady. She cannot afford evening classes.

Mrs MacFarlane bears no trace of snobbery, indeed she shows no particular awareness of social classification of any kind, and is warmly acceptant of most of the people she encounters from day to day. The kind of treachery 'class fugitives' display towards those with whom they shared their origins plays no part in Mrs MacFarlane's reasons for voting for a political party which is in fact either totally indifferent or hostile to her interests. Her political sympathies reflect, rather, a wish to emphasize her moral distance from rock bottom. Not only does she vote Conservative, but she associates the whole language of the politics of the left, its references to 'the working class', 'socialism', etc., with a degraded and dissolute world from which all moral decency has disappeared. She is caught in an ideological mystification which indissolubly associates the cure with the condition and so prevents her from criticizing the grounds of her own unhappiness.

Class injury takes another form where loving and concerned, but socially deferential, 'respectable working-class' parents bring up their children to honour middle-class values – especially educational ones – at the same time as drilling them in the art of 'knowing their place' and generally not getting ideas above their station. Products of this combination often find themselves occupying space that they feel is not rightfully theirs, living the life of a displaced person but without ever having known quite where they were displaced from.

James is a young man from just such a background. He is intelligent, sensitive and gifted. As a boy he went to the local grammar school, which he hated. He terrified his parents by becoming 'school phobic', making them despair that all their sacrifices to improve his lot in the world were about to be brought to nought by a failure of co-operation and gratitude which they just couldn't understand. But they succeeded in cajoling and bullying him into school, where he led an isolated life trying to hide from a ubiquitous middle-class gaze which as soon as it spotted him identified him as not belonging. He developed an intense interest in art, and is a very accomplished amateur painter. At seventeen he challenged his parents' supine acceptance of a social order which worked almost entirely against their interests, and even persuaded his bewildered father to join the Labour Party. But after that he ran out of steam. To be a father to his father took too much out of him for him to be able to sustain the courage to face his own world, and he has never found a job which he could tolerate. A sense of unreality and not belonging, of fraudulence and artificiality, a bitter hatred of the rat race combined with an utter lack of faith in his ability to make any impact on it leads him into deep depressions. It is not that he cannot see into the roots of his difficulties, indeed he has developed an intelligent and highly articulate critique of the world he finds himself in. The trouble is, he doesn't believe in his right to make such a critique and is sourly contemptuous of his own motives in doing so, which he sees as founded solely on weakness. He hangs on to the idea that he is 'ill' as the main bulwark between him and suicide.

James was as a child ushered into a world he was not 'bred' for, without ever being taught by his parents to believe in himself. They believed only in the world they wanted him to come to inhabit, and it never occurred to them that if he was to gain the confidence to enter it, they would have to believe in *him*. It was certainly not that they didn't love him, and they still do, though they are pained and mystified by the 'illness' which stops him profiting from all the advantages they themselves never enjoyed. And he loves them, even though the world he is now displaced into is one beyond their ken and he and they have little to say to each other.

The love James received as a child was a love largely stripped of power. Rather than gaining impetus from it, if anything it smothered and hampered him. His parents launched him into an alien world, and having pushed him off in his lonely little boat, they stood waving from a distance as he drifted gradually out of sight. This kind of isolation is often at the centre of depression. Alone in the expanses of alien territory, totally without the confidence which comes from an early infusion of parental solidarity, all the person wants to do is run for cover – dive under the bedclothes and stay there.

One may speculate whether in more ordered and stable societies – at other times, perhaps, or in other places – power relations would give rise to the same kinds of pained and confused experience I have pointed to in this chapter. Where the rules of even a positively tyrannical social order were understood and accepted as more or less immutable, its institutions might be less likely to give rise to the kinds of psychological difficulties encountered so often in 'developed' Western societies. For the operations of power in these societies are, of course, no longer feudally entrenched, but have become 'problematized'. Part of the reason for the repression of power referred to earlier is that power in all its guises has become deeply suspect, synonymous with corruption, double-dealing and oppression. The *problem*, however, is that precisely because of its repression, we are unable to confront explicitly in our relations with each other the operation of a force which cannot be excluded from them and which constitutes indeed the medium within which we exist.

We can only *pretend* to be indifferent to or detached from the wielding of power. Any society in which some must care for others, in which knowledge must be transmitted, laws enacted and enforced, will inevitably give rise to a power structure which its citizens have to operate. And some citizens, equally inevitably, will at various points in their lives and for various reasons have more power than others.

'Decent' people in our society repudiate power because they have, at least, an unexamined and unconscious sense of how much it has been abused. As far as possible, they won't truck with power. This means that all those forms of relation in which power does, whether we like it or not, play a part (as between adults and children, men and women) become confused, problematic and anarchic. This has two unfortunate consequences.

The first is that social cohesion becomes eroded to a point where everyone has to make up his or her own rules when it comes to conducting such problematic relationships. If it is not in some sense 'clear' how adults should relate to children, then a chaotic and unarticulated range of approaches to such relations will be found – anything from the use of children as sexual commodities to a kind of indifferent abandonment of them to their own devices which necessitates their growing up themselves as best they can. The difficulties and uncertainties of relations between the sexes – to be explored a little further below – need no emphasis since they are practically universally experienced by anyone trying to conduct a marriage or a 'partnership' or even simply trying to exist alongside the opposite sex in the current world.

The second unfortunate consequence of the repudiation of power is that it leaves the field completely free to those who are less squeamish; in fact, of course, nothing is more welcome to the 'discourse of power' than for the ordinary citizen to dissociate him or herself from it.

Some readers may by now be wondering uneasily whether I am about to suggest that the problematization of power calls for a 'return' to some kind of settled, authoritarian social order where everyone knows his or her place, and where, for example, class position and the condition of childhood are so tightly and universally defined that, however oppressed the occupants might be, at least their situation precludes the kind of uncertainty and confusion which gives rise to psychological distress. Obviously, however, it is the ultimate failure of these kinds of social institution which has led us to where we are now, and there can be no turning back.

Equally, though, the 'psychologizing' of 'interpersonal relations' and the development of a 'counselling culture' which suggests that the answer to our social ills lies somewhere *within* our hearts and minds, the refusal to truck with the problems of power, simply play into the interests of those at the top of our social pyramid who – whether consciously or not – are only too pleased not to have their methods come under closer scrutiny. What we need is not an unlimited supply of psychological therapy so much as the rehabilitation of politics: the realization, that is, that power can be used for good as well as for ill, and should be.

CHAPTER THREE

Bodies and Worlds – The Field of Power

We know, reflect upon and judge our world through personal experience of it. In the previous chapter I tried to illustrate the importance of social power in the shaping of ourselves and our lives, and in particular our distress, mainly by considering how its influence comes to be lived out in our personal experience. Fundamental though such experience is to our understanding of ourselves, it is, however, not the whole story: our personal view is not wide enough to take account of all the factors which contribute to a given state of affairs, and for a more complete understanding we need to stand back and consider arguments and evidence which may not be immediately given to us personally. This is, no doubt, what is meant in part by being 'scientific'.

Though some of the themes to be discussed in this chapter were introduced in the last, I want here to take a step or two back from immediate experience and to offer an account of the individual's relation to a world structured by power from a slightly more abstract and theoretical standpoint. Such an account is needed, I believe, in order to give greater depth and breadth to our understanding of the ways in which personal distress is generated in a world over which we as individuals have very little control. (Much of what follows is summarized more formally in the Appendix to this book.)

TRADITIONAL APPROACHES

Those branches of psychology – the so-called 'psychodynamic' approaches – which have concerned themselves centrally with 'mental disorder', or emotional distress, while differing widely in the types of theory they put forward to explain the 'clinical phenomena', tend to share a basic methodology. This starts out with individual adults in distress (usually encountered first in some form of one-to-one 'treatment') and works back from there to postulate supposedly fundamental psychological mechanisms or processes which have led to the 'clinical picture'. In this way the reflective clinician – Sigmund Freud, say, or Carl Rogers – is confronted by a number of complex, socially highly developed individuals who in fact exist as, so to speak, finished articles in a social and cultural setting which they share with the clinician. What the latter then looks for are characteristics which mark these individuals out from other people not considered clinically 'abnormal', and which might point to processes whereby they came to be the way they are. The focus is thus the person ('patient', 'client') and what is assumed to be going on, or to have gone on, 'inside' him or her.

The clinician's consulting room becomes a microcosm supposedly containing all the explanatory material necessary for an adequate theory of 'psychopathology'. The clinician occupies the centre of this microcosmic world as a kind of nonpathological scientific wizard, able to identify and expose the processes leading to the patient's disorder and manipulate them such that the abnormalities are repaired. What tends to get left out of account, since it is so difficult not to take for granted, is the situation – the world – in which *both* clinician *and* patient find themselves. This is a bit like goldfish constructing a theoretical explanation of their condition solely from the data available to them in their bowl: some important and useful observations would doubtless get made, but rather a lot would be left out. The implications of this for the process of psychotherapy itself will be considered in more detail in Chapter Five.

In the end, of course, our scientific understanding is always going to be limited by the horizon of our field of vision: no 'complete' explanation, could there be such a thing, will ever be available to us of anything. But failure to look out of the consulting room window to the world beyond has led to some unnecessary shortsightedness in much psychological and psychotherapeutic theorizing. At least three common mistakes come quickly to mind:

1. Taking insufficient account of a wider world – of the microcosm's being located in a macrocosm – makes it more likely that the clinician will 'pathologize' patients, i.e., will be focally aware of what makes them 'different' rather than of how patients *and* clinician are at the mercy of and shaped by forces which dwarf the events and preoccupations of their individual lives. This error is very nearly universal in the most widely accepted approaches to 'mental illness'. It helps establish a cultural dimension of normality-abnormality which has the most profound and wide-ranging implications for social organization – for example, in determining who are considered competent members of our society and what should be the appropriate means of their 'treatment' or 'management' if they are not. It encourages us to distinguish between each other on the grounds of personal competence or 'mental health' rather than forging solidarity between us in our struggles with the problems presented to us by a hard world.

2. The somewhat claustrophobic concentration on the 'inner lives' of people who have both the self-concern and the resources to seek out individual psychotherapy tends to lead – as it did, for example, in the case of Freudian psychoanalysis – to an elaborate structure of theoretical concepts, many of them wonderful and some of them weird, which the clinician has to postulate in order to keep pace with the complexity of the phenomena which a thoughtful, well-educated and, literally, resourceful adult can present. Hence the appearance on the

theoretical scene of 'unconscious minds', 'ids', 'egos', 'complexes', 'personas', 'animas', and so on. Hence the emphasis in many psychotherapies on internal worlds, inner resources, responsibility and choice, the power in one guise or another of positive thinking. The trouble is that, though no doubt they point to features of human conduct and understanding of great importance, such theoretical constructs have a vagueness, and a tendency to proliferate, that obscure the more fundamental processes which operate beyond the microcosm; they may have a kind of magical seductiveness, an attractive pseudoauthority, but they do not have the generally applicable precision which can be used in any acceptably (nondogmatically) systematic way. This is one reason why no real science of psychology has emerged, but only a collection of competing, semi-patented, 'brand name' approaches.

3. Restriction to the microcosm of the consulting room leads clinicians to overestimate the importance of their own activity in 'curing' patients' problems. This overestimation of the therapist's role has led at times to expressions of therapeutic self-importance almost embarrassing in their absurdity and no doubt damaging to those – particularly patients – who have been either bullied or seduced into taking them seriously (Jeffrey Masson's *Against Therapy* is an enlightening source of examples).

Freud, for instance, issued pompous advice to his patients that they should not make major changes to the circumstances of their lives while 'under analysis', and the theoretical centrality of the 'transference relationship' in psychoanalysis – the notion that the analyst becomes, so to speak, the symbolic centre of the patient's universe – inflates the figure of the analyst in relation to the wider environment such that it overshadows absolutely everything else that happens in the patient's life.

More subtly, the exclusive concentration on what happens in the therapeutic microcosm tends to overemphasize the curative powers of the therapist even where the latter is not represented theoretically as anything other than averagely human. In his

Client-Centred Therapy, for example, Carl Rogers gave central importance to the quality of the relationship between patient and therapist – the well-known triad of 'warmth, empathy and genuineness'. However, while there is no doubt that, in accounting for what goes on in the consulting room, attention to such factors is an advance on the mysteries of the 'transference', still left out of account is the fact that the therapist is only a very small part of the world in which both therapist and patient find themselves.

BEHAVIOURAL APPROACHES

Not all approaches within the broadly 'clinical' field have been quite as entangled in the complicated phenomena of the consulting room when putting together a theoretical account of distress. Apart from those which have taken their main impetus from medicine and which incline therefore to an essentially biological account of distress (and so end up with the pills, potions and electric shocks of psychiatry), the most important are the behavioural approaches. At bottom, behaviourism suggested that we react the way we do because of what happens to us in the environment surrounding us. There is in my view a lot to be said for this transparently simple claim. The trouble is, it was always connected by behaviourists to an extremely blinkered view of what people, environments, 'stimuli' and 'responses' actually were, and adopted an unbelievably simplistic dogma concerning what it means to be 'scientific' while insisting with positively inquisitorial fanaticism that scientific is what we all had to be. As is well known, behaviourism attached itself limpet-like to the doctrines of Ivan Pavlov, the Russian physiologist, who generalized the reactions of experimental dogs to the various predicaments devised for them in his laboratories into a 'conditioning' theory of learning which eventually found its way into clinical psychology in the West (and, indeed, is still to be found there, even if modified out of almost all recognition).

The advantage of behaviourism was that it attempted to escape the complications of making the inside of an adult human being's head the starting point for a theory of psychological functioning. Instead of diving straight into the complexities of 'thought', 'imagery', 'will', 'instinct', etc., behaviourists were attracted to the simpler course – long established in the Anglo-Saxon philosophical tradition – of trying to understand human conduct as an interaction of person ('organism') and environment. The fact that behaviourism almost immediately got swept into painful oversimplifications of the processes involved was partly no doubt a function of the utilitarian scientism of the time, but that it eventually became lost in rationally indefensible authoritarian dogma should not deter us from trying to rescue the theoretical tradition which, even if only momentarily, it kept alive. This is what may perhaps be called the environmentalist tradition: the idea that a human being is the product of a body and a world, i.e., two essentially material structures, out of which the more intangible phenomena of psychology emerge.

THE IMPORTANCE OF THE ENVIRONMENT

My aim here cannot be to set out a grandiose theory of 'psychology'. What I do want to do is to sketch out the features of an environmentalist-materialist approach which are most essential to an understanding of emotional distress and confusion (especially, of course, distress and confusion which are usually thought of as 'abnormal' or 'pathological' in some way). There is not a great deal of point in theorizing for the sake of it; the reasons for its being necessary at this point are a) because, as I've indicated, the current orthodoxy ignores almost totally issues such as power which are crucial to our understanding, and b) because a reasonably accurate theoretical account leads to deepening insight into the phenomena concerned and to new ways of thinking about and handling them.

We start out with nothing more complicated than a human body in a world (environment) as shown in figure 1. In other

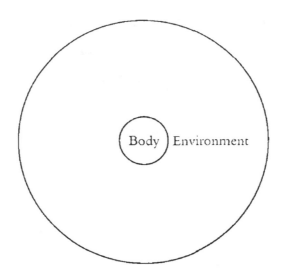

FIGURE 1: The raw materials

words, to account for the inarticulate distress of someone trying to understand and give a coherent picture of the misery he or she feels, one will always refer back in the end to features either of human biology or of the environment(s) in which those biological processes are or were once taking place. (Medicine, of course, places nearly all its eggs in the biological basket, whereas in what follows I shall be putting much heavier emphasis on environmental factors.) In common with the behaviourists, we have no need to import as *basic* components into our theoretical structure such entities as immortal souls, unconscious minds, ids, egos, faculties of will, instincts, or any other of the nonmaterial, 'internal' features of people which it is so difficult not to credit them with as we encounter them as 'finished products' in our everyday lives.

A human body abstracted from its environment is not a person: it is merely a collection of all the biological bits and pieces which go to make up bodies. A person only comes into being when a body is placed in a social world which interacts with it.

As is suggested by the hatched area in figure 2, a person is by no means identical with the material structures of his or her body, but is a construct of the interaction between body and

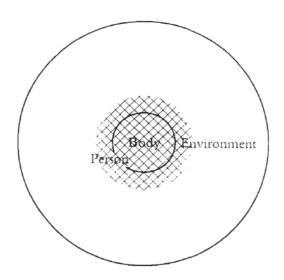

FIGURE 2: The person as interaction between body and environment

but is a construct of the interaction between body and environment. A person is partly body, certainly, but is also partly environment. For example, a body may make vocal noises – it certainly has the potentiality to utter, but the *language* which a *person* comes to be able to speak, and in a sense 'possesses', is in the social environment entirely outside the body. Part of what it means to be a person is being able to communicate, and that I speak English certainly seems like being part of 'me' as a person, but it is not enclosed somehow inside my skin – it stretches out into the world around 'me'. Or to put it another way, the world outside extends its social institutions and practices into 'me': 'I' am the hatched area which is neither body nor world, but a complex interaction of both.

THE POVERTY OF INDIVIDUALISM

All this may strike the reader as tiresomely abstract. There is, however, an issue of the very profoundest importance to be recognized at this stage before it becomes overlaid by some of the considerations to ensue. This is that an 'individual' person is, in fact, not individual at all in anything much other than the actual space in the world he or she occupies and the experience this inevitably gives rise to (nobody else can experience exactly what you do if only because nobody else can stand exactly where you are). Part of what an 'individual' consists of is precisely nonindividual, social conventions, practices, meanings and institutions which we all share in common. We are, of course, individual bodies in the sense that mine is a different body from yours (but even here our bodies are remarkably similar – a fact which it will be important to consider later on). When, then, we come to examine a person's individual experience (our particular interest being, of course, *distressing* experience) we are likely to be misled if we conceive of its causes and cures purely as an 'individual' matter. We need always, that is, to keep an eye on those aspects of our so-called 'individuality' which are in fact features of a world we have in common.

I do not wish – indeed am not competent – to consider in any detail the specifically biological contribution to personhood of the body-world interaction. There can be no doubt that the nature of our embodiment – whether, for example, as male/female, light/heavy, tall/short, strong/weak, quick/slow, and many much more subtle distinctions than these – contributes crucially to our interaction with the world and experience of life. In these respects also genetic structures cannot but be of fundamental importance. However, while I in no sense see our biology as irrelevant to an account of our personhood, the contribution of the environment does seem to me overwhelmingly more significant for an understanding of the kind of phenomena of distress with which I am centrally concerned. From this aspect it seems to me most important to try to redress the balance in favour of environmental factors which even 'environmentalist' approaches such as behaviourism have failed to establish.

For the behaviourist, in fact, the 'environment' consists of little more than bundles of positively and negatively charged 'stimuli' or 'reinforcements' which spring into life, so it seems, from a completely unanalysed, (presumably) social world whose contents and concerns are left utterly mysterious. It is this world above all which needs elucidation.

The Nature of the Environment

From the standpoint of the individual, the environment consists of a practically limitless field of influence and a much more limited field of opportunity. There are, that is to say, a whole range of influences which bear down and ultimately impinge upon the individual, and a limited range of actions available to him or her by means of which he or she may exert some influence back into the environment. Influence may thus impinge on the person *intransitively* (i.e., 'stopping with' the person and resulting, perhaps, in suffering or pleasure) or *transitively* (i.e., being transformed *through* the individual into personal action of some kind). The environment is ordered according to the dimensions of space and time and organized by power. One could say, indeed, that the environment *is* social space–time and that power is the essential principle giving it motion and structure.

A person's 'state of mind' is thus explainable in principle through an understanding of the influences operating in the environmental space in which he or she is located. It is important not to overlook the dimension of time: not only is there a current set of influences bearing down upon the person, but there have also been former sets of influences, so that the person is shaped by a history as well as by present circumstances (time may be represented by extending the circular diagram in figure 2, page 63, into the cylindrical one in figure 3, page 74). Environmental influence has, then, a dimension of time which runs most essentially from past to present, and a spatial dimension which, as anticipated in Chapter Two, I think is best characterized as proximal/distal. For the sake of clarity I shall consider these dimensions of space and time separately, though, of course, in practice they cannot be totally abstracted from each other.

ENVIRONMENTAL SPACE

In everyday life the influences operating in the environment cannot but be experienced as close up against the person. Indeed, ultimately they form a part of bodily experience as sensations. Our experience of life is given to us through our immediate relations with others at home, at work, at school, and in our social and recreational activities. There is therefore an inevitable 'proximity' about our most immediate and potent experience. However, the reasons for the events which happen, so to speak, right up against our skin, may – in most cases will – be located much further away in the environmental power structure. One may or may not have insight into these. Education, access to accurate analysis by those better placed than ourselves, and so on, may help to clarify the distal reasons for our proximal experience, and such access therefore becomes in itself a form of power because it gives us a degree of (only potential) control over what happens to us.

For most people, 'reality' is the proximal world of their immediate experience. They tend to be indifferent to, or even impatient with, analyses of their experience which refer to distal events or influences because these may seem – may indeed be – so uncertain and speculative. They therefore tend to attribute 'the cause' of how they feel to the proximal experience of events or the actions of people close to them which are in fact determined by distal influences well out of their sight.

Geoff has worked for eighteen years in a factory now owned by an international conglomerate of vast proportions. In a hurry to get home after a late shift he runs past the security guard (whom he's known and chatted to in the canteen for the past eight years), who shouts something after him. He gives the guard a wave, jumps into his car and drives off. As soon as he arrives at work next day he is questioned for an hour about his refusal to stop for a spot check on the previous night. At first he jokes about it with the security personnel as he has a spotless record and is confident of his reputation. However, he is finally marched into a manager's office and told formally to account for himself. He is told that disobeying an order to stop for a check is a sackable offence. After an uneasy week's wait he is summoned before an official he has not seen before and summarily dismissed. 'I'm not interested in what you've got to say,' this official tells him, 'so far as I'm concerned you're just a number. You're fired.' This minor functionary, hired no doubt to spare local managers a hatchery which might prove counterproductive, is described by Geoff as 'the top man from London', and his account suggests that local union officials view his power in similarly awe-struck terms. At any rate, Geoff feels himself up against forces far too powerful for him to challenge, and all his distress centres round the mystifying treachery of the security guard he had considered a friend, the cruel and unjust impugning of his honesty by a firm he had worked for for so long, wild frustration at being unable to establish his innocence, and a nagging sense of guilt at finding his character blackened. Like many people who have in one way or another been abused by power, he feels literally dirty. After three months of sleeplessness, anxiety and distress, he finds another job: 'longer hours and less money, but at least I've got my self-respect back'. Geoff gets little comfort from the knowledge that the factory was running at a loss and needed to 'rationalize' by shedding staff as cheaply as possible (summary dismissal being the cheapest and quickest method). His 'self-respect' was inextricably bound up with his proximal relations at work and could not be rescued through an abstract understanding of the distal operations of international finance.

THE POWER HORIZON

The idea, introduced in the previous chapter, that each of us exists within a 'power horizon' is extremely important to an understanding both of the inaccuracy of much of our moralizing and psychologizing – professional as well as amateur – about why people act as they do, and of the use to which such inaccuracy may be put by those wishing unscrupulously to augment their power. In accounting for our experience of the world, and not least for the pain and distress which comes to be registered physically on our bodies, we tend to tell ourselves endless, often conflicting stories. We revise and revise again our constructions of what we see as the 'motives' of those around us as well as the (usually more creditable!) motives we detect within ourselves. Just as Geoff was stuck with trying to account for the motives of his friend the security guard, we all tend to rummage around inside the supposed 'inner space' of those we encounter in everyday life until we find a 'reason' for what they do which gives us at least temporary satisfaction.

Psychology and philosophy themselves postulate countless variants on the theme of 'motive', 'impulse', 'will', 'responsibility', etc., all of which similarly seek proximal causes for actions which, in fact, can only be accounted for within a very much wider environmental power structure. It is scarcely surprising that accounts of human motivation are often attended by references to its mysterious nature, since as long as one insists on locating the reasons for their actions *inside* people, mysterious is what they're bound to remain: in fact, there *is* no inside of a kind which will accommodate lurking motives. The 'mystery' of the human soul and its supposed motivational component is in my view no mystery at all, but rather the projection inwards (i.e., into an 'inner space' which actually doesn't exist) of an *outer* mystery which is indeed very real.

Both our own actions and the actions of those around us may be mysterious not because we cannot penetrate the depths of each other's inner worlds, unconscious minds, etc., but because we simply cannot see over the power horizons which limit our view of the causes of things. We are thus restricted to telling ourselves stories, making guesses, speculating and surmising about happenings in our proximal worlds which have distal causes well out of sight. Such distal causes set off complex concatenations of events which reverberate throughout large segments of social environmental space and end up registering on our senses through the mediation of one or several people close to us. Much of the time, therefore, we remain in the dark not only about the reasons for the conduct of others, but equally about our own conduct.

Nobody (other than an entirely hypothetical deity) has a limitless power horizon, though people differ widely in the depth of the power horizons which enclose the various spheres in which they lead their existence. As I have already noted, it is frequently in the interests of those with a greater vista of power deliberately to limit as far as they can what others are able to see. One way of doing this is to make use of the nearly irresistible appeal of proximal explanation. Thus the government minister eager to discount the socioeconomic causes of urban rioting will invoke an (utterly mysterious) 'criminality', or absence of 'parental discipline', to account for it. Much closer to home, we are likely in our domestic disputes with each other endlessly (if usually profoundly unsatisfactorily) to attribute personal spites (to others) and virtues (to ourselves) as reasons for our friction which in fact has causes located far off in the networks of power.

I shall be considering issues to do with the kinds of professional help which may be of use to people in distress in Chapter Five, but it is worth noting at this point that a particular difficulty confronting people who wish to change how they feel is that their feelings are often likely to be related to events which, because they are taking place over their power horizon, they cannot even see – and even if they could they would be likely still to find it quite beyond their powers to do anything about them. And when one takes the dimension of time into account, things get even more difficult.

ENVIRONMENTAL TIME

Most approaches to psychotherapy and clinical psychology rely on one version or another of a theory of 'insight' which assumes that once one has identified the origin of one's 'pathological'

conduct or experience, one can make the adjustments necessary
to return to normality. That in their clinical experience this does
not in fact seem to happen has led some theorists to acknowledge
the inadequacy of merely 'intellectual' insight, and to proclaim
instead the superiority of 'emotional insight'. A change of mind,
it seems, is less effective than a change of heart.

However, I think the situation is considerably more difficult
than would be suggested by any approach relying on one form
or another of the concept of 'insight', which seems to me a good
example of the kind of essentially unanalysable and magical process
to which therapeutic psychologies so often appeal. Events which
have happened in the past to make someone the kind of person
he or she is do not just present the kinds of problems of access
of distal events happening in the present; they are completely
beyond reach.

The illusion of accessibility to the past – greatly and to my
mind illegitimately exploited by 'cognitive' psychologies which
place heavy therapeutic emphasis on the reinterpretation of history
– is probably maintained by an unexamined assumption most of
us have that the past somehow exists in the present as memories
in some form of internal space. It may easily seem to us that we
can reach into this space, shuffle its contents around and so set
in train a chain of readjustments which will lead to a radical
difference in the way we feel now.

Interestingly, it is felt that such retrospective adjustments are
possible only in those matters of what one might call character
which are typically subject to moral scrutiny and debate; nobody
is likely to assume that the more solid and indisputable
achievements of past learning – such as language acquisition or
the possession of particular practical abilities – are open to the
same kind of interior tinkering. While it might be thought that
I can examine my past and revise my reasons for being hostile
or anxious, nobody expects me to be able – however expedient
it might be – to forget my knowledge of English and acquire
one of Chinese merely by recalling the circumstances of my

learning the former and reflecting on the desirability of knowing the latter.

In fact, a person's experience at any point along the dimension of time is acquired as part of a bodily interaction with the proximal effects of distal causes. The experience itself may seem to exist insubstantially but somehow accessibly in one's head, but in truth it is organically embodied: becomes, that is, physically part of ourselves. The past leaves its marks upon us in various degrees of intensity and durability – as I suggested in the last chapter the impress of power can be extremely long-lasting – but we have no real say in the matter, and cannot choose what forms of embodied experience we wish to retain and what to erase. Once I have learned to ride a bicycle or play the piano I cannot choose to forget, though of course such abilities may fade with the course of time.

THE REHABILITATION OF 'CHARACTER'

The idea that we are in large part the products of a past which we can do nothing to change – not to mention a present whose influences are well out of reach – suggests to me that it would be valuable to resurrect a concept of 'character' which has largely disappeared from psychology. 'Character' gave way to 'personality', which in turn splintered into various subsets of 'behaviours', 'cognitive styles', and so on, which appeared increasingly to permit of professional intervention: a human being becomes split into manipulable bits and pieces, which can be adjusted and reassembled in accordance with some normative ideal. One can see, of course, what's in this for psychology, but as an accurate conceptualization of what it is to be a person, it leaves a lot to be desired.

In fact, people are the people that they are by reason of the things which have happened to them and the nature of the world in which they are currently having to live their lives. We are characters shaped by a past world and struggling with a current world which, absolutely inevitably, we can understand only imperfectly. Shuffling the contents of our heads may have all sorts of rewards and fascinations, but it will do very little to make us other than we are.

The difference between what psychology can achieve and what it has always hoped to achieve is the difference between self-discovery and self-invention. We can up to a point discover what kinds of characters we are, but we cannot choose to be the 'personalities' we should like to be, any more than we can choose to be Olympic athletes or concert violinists. In maintaining this I am, of course, running directly counter to that very considerable section of the psychotherapy and 'personal growth' industry which promises one form or another of self-choice. Such a promise can only be made, however, through wilful ignorance of a power-structured world in which even the concept of free will is no more than a necessary illusion.

It becomes important at this point to consider in a little more detail the nature of the powers which organize that world.

TYPES OF POWER

Sociologists tend to agree in differentiating three types of power which give order to our relations with each other[1]: coercive, economic and ideological power. Individuals thus find themselves at the centre of a network of social influences which are applied either as brute force, money power, or through the manipulation and control of the meaning systems by which we make sense of the world. While the point is usually made that these three forms of power are essentially independent of each other – i.e., that it is possible to possess one form without having access to either of the other two – in practice they are, of course, often related. When all else fails it is power over the body – physical coercion – which virtually guarantees the achievement of the aims of the

1. See, for example, W. G. Runciman, *A Treatise on Social Theory*, Vol. II, Cambridge Univeristy Press, 1989.

powerful (though the *means* of force, especially on an international scale, may well be dependent on wealth).

While brute force might be the ultimate sanction, the more subtle application of ideological power is likely to be far more effective in controlling large segments of society: if citizens can be brought to believe that their government consists of public-spirited men and women who have at heart only the welfare of society as a whole, things are likely to go far more smoothly than where a 'band of brigands', to borrow Robert Tressell's phrase[2], fails to conceal its designs from an exploited populace and has consequently to resort to brutal repression. The more a government can control the beliefs and perceptions of significant sections of society, the less likely will be its need for control over their bodies.

The Field of Power

The processes, or meaning systems (in this and much of what follows it may help the reader to refer to figure 3), which mediate a person's experience, for example, his or her beliefs about the nature of the world and the social events occurring in it, are derived partly from physical interaction with the environment – the pleasurable sensation of benign influences and the painful sensation of malign ones – and partly, probably mainly, from interaction with the socially established categories of meaning which are firmly in place in the world well in advance of the individual's occupancy of it. To make sense of what we directly, physically experience, we are heavily dependent on the explanations and meanings afforded us by our culture. Our personal assimilation to, and adaptation of, these meaning systems is roughly what is meant by our 'psychology'. It cannot be emphasized too strongly (since it is an error so often made) that this psychology, all those linguistic and nonlinguistic systems for

2. From his *The Ragged-Trousered Philanthropists*.

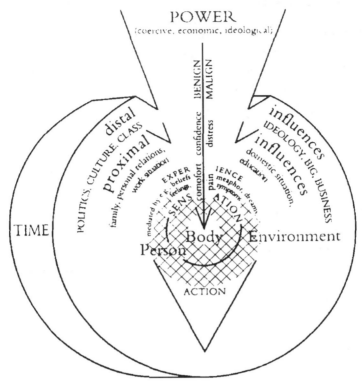

FIGURE 3: The field of power

making sense of the world – thought, memory, dreams, perceptions, feelings, etc. – do not exist independently of the environment of which indeed they are partly constituted. Our psychology is not ours to manipulate at will and we cannot detach it from the social powers which hold it in place.

This means that having, for example, recognized the importance of people's beliefs or 'attitudes' as regulators of their conduct, we cannot somehow isolate them like the printed circuits of an electronic machine and slide them in and out of people in the expectation of achieving 'behaviour change'. For an attitude is not a personal possession in the way that a toe, or an ear, or an appendix is; it is linked to and partly produced by a network of social forces which may stretch out to the most distal cultural powers. It is control of those powers *outside* people which ultimately achieves control of people themselves.

The explanation of individual experience and conduct is, then, to be sought in a complex set of social interactions in which the most likely pattern is for extremely powerful distal events – political or economic perhaps – to reverberate through a network of influence and interest until they work themselves out in the proximal relations which make up the context of the individual's personal life. These in turn will be mediated physically as sensations (pain and pleasure) and psychologically via the meaning systems acquired by the person in social space-time. Geoff's distress was attributed by him mostly to his immediate contact with people where he worked, stretching out only as far as the 'top man from London', and partly to an inarticulate (ideologically determined) sense of personal inadequacy and guilt. In fact, of course, if certain events in far distant boardrooms had not reverberated down through systems of accounting and chains of management, Geoff would still be working where he was.

It seems self-evident that the social structure of power is pyramidal, that essentially the story is one of control of the many by the few. I have already remarked that one of the most important tasks of ideological power is to obscure the workings of this process, and it is indeed striking how difficult it is to obtain any reasonably clear picture of where power originates in society. The mass media are, of course, very little help, not least because they themselves *constitute* ideological power and are owned and controlled by people and groups whose whole purpose (whether or not they are aware of it) is to contain ordinary mortals' understanding of the social processes of power within as proximal a compass as possible.

Moralizing and psychologizing are the stock in trade of those whose interest it is to narrow the power horizon of the average citizen, and so the language used is a relentlessly proximal one of motive and blame rather than cause and effect. The mass media wield their ideological power in an effort to define reality, not to explore and expose its nature. Even scholarly sociological enquiry seems not to be able to penetrate with any clarity the obscurity shrouding the upper reaches of the pyramid of power. Exactly who the powerful are tends to be dimly suggested in fleeting glimpses – as of the chimneys of an enormous mansion rising just discernibly from a copse at the end of a miles-long avenue closed off by discreetly placed electronic gates – or faint flickerings of insight as one senses the extraordinary linkages between political power, big business, large-scale corruption and international crime.

However all this may be (I lay no claim to an especially extended power horizon!), it would seem likely to be a mistake to assume that, in view of its undoubtedly pyramidal structure, power is essentially a personal matter. For tyrants must always remain nervously vulnerable to the very fact of their singularity, whether exerting distal power through the possession of vast personal fortunes or the command of private armies, or the merely proximal power of physical bullying: their power is in truth no more reliable than the proverbial assassin's bullet allows it to be. Power is much more usually, and effectively, gained and maintained through association with others and through an institutional structuration of influence which affords real stability to the powers possessed. Thus, while power in terms of the quantum available to each individual is indeed likely to be distributed pyramidally, it is also the case that people located higher up the pyramid are more likely to be embedded in a relatively stable structure of power involving other people than are those at the bottom. In other words, the really powerful individual, far from being the kind of isolated, power-crazed megalomaniac depicted in the popular literature of paranoia (by Ian Fleming, for example), is in fact more likely to be someone who is located in a network of institutionalized, formal (legally established) and informal (private 'clubs' of one kind or another) powers and privileges.

Those who truly stand in isolation are the people at the bottom of the power pyramid, so stripped of any kind of institutional or socially shared power that they are reduced in the final analysis to the utterly proximal powers afforded by their mere existence as embodied individuals: for a man this may mean recourse to brute force, for a woman to the bartering of her sexuality. (There is a kind of microcosmic theoretical purity about the relation of the prostitute to her pimp which illuminates a great deal of the less palatable aspect of the wider social organization. Reduced to the very dregs of the proximal power available to her, the prostitute is still vulnerable to the sheer muscle power of the pimp who effects a takeover of her business.)

THE MEDIATION OF POWER

Power is transmitted through networks of associative groups, each group seeking to maximize its interest and preserve its advantage. The coercive power of totalitarian regimes is maintained through armies and the secret police; big business operates through a managerial bureaucracy; various kinds of cultural advantage are preserved through a range of educational, scientific and technical, professional groups and institutions; class advantage, as I illustrated in the last chapter, is maintained by a caste system of distinction. Each such grouping or section of society tries to maintain its position by developing exclusive methods of training and selection for admission, specialized procedures and activities mysterious to the uninitiated, esoteric languages largely unintelligible to outsiders, and so on. To belong to such a group usually confers a degree of power on the individual which he or she would not otherwise have, and so he or she develops almost instantaneously an interest in the group's continued existence and a commitment to contributing as much as possible to its stability. The rigour with which even supposedly disinterested social institutions – for example, in education or science – discipline their members, and the readiness of the members themselves to submerge their individuality in adopting the procedures and jargon of the group, testify to their mutual dependence in maintaining an interest which places them at an advantage in relation to the mass of society.

Keeping control of meaning is of central importance to the preservation of power, and this, of course, is the essence of ideology. As Michel Foucault argues so persuasively in *Discipline and Punish*, the construction and maintenance of an apparatus of largely ideological power is a very much more effective way of organizing and controlling mass society than is simple recourse to brute force, and it is through a positive fog of ideology that most of us have to stumble our way towards the truth. There are, of course, a thousand ways of keeping ideological control (or, as Dorothy Rowe puts it, of bamboozling people): officially through the established institutions of religion, education and 'therapy', unofficially through mass media, which are able to shape the very 'reality' we can see and talk about. Enormous power can be gained through the appropriation of meaning itself: to impose a language on all which is interpretable by only a small élite is the ultimate in the exercise of ideological power. Priests and doctors have at different times and to different extents come close to perfecting this technique, but most professional groups are more or less adept at it.

It is important to note that the power of ideology stems from the *social* nature of meaning. To control meaning is to gain power through *associating* with some people in ascendancy over other people. Altering or adjusting 'meanings' as they exist individually as beliefs, attitudes or perceptions in your or my head is of comparatively little significance. The difference between ideological power and impotent magic is that the former is public and social and the latter is private and individual; the former gives real power over people, the latter only a spurious, wishful illusion of power. It is equivalent to the difference between learning a real language (which gives access to real social powers and possibilities) and inventing a private one (which merely locks one into autistic, essentially crazy self-communion). It is in many ways the tradition of magic that survives in those brands of psychology and psychotherapy which advocate tinkering with the individual's personal systems of meaning within the microenvironment of the consulting room; unless the *social* significance of the individual's psychology can be taken fully into account (a question to be addressed further in Chapter Five), such tinkering will achieve nothing of substance.

Almost no adult individual is totally powerless, if only because, as I have indicated, he or she may have recourse to the powers afforded by embodiment. While such power may at times reach a zenith of quite spectacular violence, it is still in the overall scale of things extremely puny, and will be called upon with any regularity only by the socially least advantaged members of society. The power afforded by the simple act of association with others is very much more effective, and for this reason alone the more powerful are always likely to seek to limit the extent to which the less powerful are able to form associations of any kind. The most obvious example is the inclination of employers in a capitalist society to limit the process and powers of unionization, but it is in the interest of any group with claims to power (for example, the professions) to keep dependent on it (for 'advice', 'treatment', or whatever) people who are as far as possible isolated from each other.

The more 'private' and 'individual' people become, the more detached they will be from the possibility of acquiring associative power – indeed such power is likely to become available to them only through association with some sort of 'professional', a lawyer or therapist, for example, or in the confined domesticity of their personal lives (hence, no doubt, the central concern most people have in present-day culture with 'relationships'; hence also the eagerness of some politicians to extol the sanctity of 'the family' and to represent it as the largest viable social building block). For most people these days, 'solidarity' – the participation in associative power – is limited to a 'relationship' with just one or two people. This, of course, provides the optimally extended base of the power pyramid for exploitation by its higher levels.

THE MYSTIFICATION OF POWER

The need for association with powerful others, first experienced in the child's relations with the adults around it, is observable most poignantly in those instances where it is most exploited. It is, for example, easy to react with contempt or incredulity to the apparently utterly trivial preoccupations of the popular press, but, in fact, it thrives upon the provision of a mystified version of the need for associative power – 'mystified' because the power actually yielded is very nearly nil. For associative power becomes itself a marketable product. 'Celebrities' and 'personalities' permit their own, often quite considerable social power to be exploited through encouraging a degree of intimacy with the 'little people' who read in magazines and tabloids of their private concerns, conduct and relationships. The reader is allowed to become the confidant of the 'celebrity', perhaps recreating thereby an echo of the warmth once gained from the trust of a parent, and so comes into possession of 'knowledge' which offers a pathetically false promise of increased social standing, especially presumably among those not so favoured.

The seductiveness of such marketed power is that it appears to be freely offered by the celebrity – the reader is invited into his or her confidence. The 'star' who 'tells' willingly whom she is sleeping with gives her confidant privileged access to her world as to a friend. Where, on the other hand, such intimacies are revealed through the treachery of a former butler or extorted by trickery and the telephoto lens, the knowledge gained seems more like the knowledge of a spy: shameful but potentially useful. Exploitation of the phenomena of power by association is, of course, well recognized by those who need to maintain and augment their ideological capital by patronizing the powerless and cultivating their interest. Almost everyone can feel part of the Royal Family if the ideological machinery is tended carefully enough, and if the paparazzi didn't exist, the rich and famous would have to invent them.

The power actually conferred by mystified association with the powerful is, of course, nonexistent in the sense of the individual's becoming a real intimate of the 'celebrity'. However, it may perhaps do a very little to augment social solidarity between those 'in the know', if only because it gives them something to talk about together. A fan club, for example, might offer people opportunities for association with each other much more valuable than the association each might *feel* they had with the object of their veneration.

Religion seems sometimes to work like this, and, when it does, provides a good example of the contrast between the inaccuracy of personal beliefs based on proximal experience and the more complete account offered by a distal view. I have, for example, encountered several people for whom attachment to one form or other of fundamentalist, 'born again' Christianity has resulted in greatly increased happiness and indeed in their ability to gain some control in areas of their lives where they had been feeling particularly helpless and lost. Not surprisingly, they tend to attribute such improvement to their newly cemented relationship with Jesus, rather as if they had found an especially powerful friend ready to lend them a receptive ear at any time of need, and poised to put at their disposal his virtually limitless resources should the request be sufficiently earnestly made. This seems to me a false belief not only in respect of there being no such friend, but also in there being no real efficacy to the *belief* that one has such a friend (on its own, i.e., out of a context of association with others, such a belief would constitute madness).

While those forms of psychology which have failed to detach themselves from their roots in magic would be ready enough to acknowledge the power of beliefs of this kind, it seems to me much more plausible that their potency lies in the social solidarity which *sharing* them brings about. In every instance that I can think of what has made the difference to the previously isolated and despairing, now born-again-Christian person has not been any special relationship with God (which is merely the story people tell themselves) but an empowering association (solidarity) with a group of like-minded others who are prepared to endorse that story.

'SELF-CONTROL' - INSIDE AND OUTSIDE

The great error – one might even say the fundamental flaw – of psychology has been to consider individual meaning-systems as somehow belonging to and in the control of the people of whom they form a part. Over and over again the assumption is made that things like beliefs and attitudes are located *inside* a person and that, while they may indeed be seen as guiding his or her conduct, they are also, in some way which is almost always left mysterious, subject to operations of his or her will. Thus, if the person sees fit – perhaps through a process of having gained 'insight' – he or she can in some sense 'decide' to alter beliefs or attitudes which have now come to be seen as inappropriate or inconvenient.

Despite having a long and honourable pedigree, particularly in British philosophy, the idea that we are *not* in fact in charge of ourselves in this way is for most people still very difficult to grasp, mainly because it has become ideologically so obscured. Furthermore, those approaches to psychology, such as behaviourism, which have challenged the view that we have total moral control over ourselves have so over-simplified the issues as to discredit the core of their own intellectual enterprise.

What one has to do, it seems to me, is emphasize once again that the 'person' is not a bounded entity separated off from the world in which he or she exists, but an interaction of body with world, consisting partially of both. People cannot control their beliefs and attitudes because people *are* their beliefs and attitudes. Beliefs and attitudes, as well as the nonverbal meaning-systems like dream and metaphor which order our experience, are *constituents* of our personhood: there is no further 'person' who can somehow step outside this constituency, adjust it, and then step back in again.

What seems like our 'inside' – what psychologists so often refer to as the 'self', 'inner space', etc. – does not exist in any material sense. Nor does it 'exist' in any immaterial sense – it is, rather, a way of referring to our self-consciousness. Exactly as we can talk to, as well as about, others we can talk to and about ourselves (though perhaps with differing degrees of honesty) concerning our experience of the world. We can talk about the various ways in which we interact bodily with the world, we can sense things about it, we can dream about, describe and reflect upon it with varying degrees of clarity, accuracy, skill or grace, but we do not necessarily control it thereby. What makes a difference to the way we are, what changes us or permits us to change, is not the voluntary manipulation of inner resources (for there is no 'inner') but the influence of or access to *outer* resources and powers. Neither 'self' nor world can be influenced or changed by anything other than the exercise of power.

This is not to say that we do not as individuals possess personal resources – clearly any such claim would be ludicrous – but that it is seriously misleading to characterize such resources as 'inner', since as soon as we start unreflectively to entertain such a notion, we lay the foundation for a moralistic calculus of 'personal worth' and so on. What people tend to see as 'inner resources' are most usually *outer* resources which they have acquired over time. The idea of an 'inner world' is in this way the transmutation of a temporal phenomenon into a spatial metaphor.

My propensity to meet threat without anxiety ('confidence' or 'courage'), no differently from my ability to speak French, is something I have learned or been enabled or empowered to do at some previous point of my existence. I can no more summon confidence up from some kind of inner space than I can a knowledge of French if I have not acquired them from the outer world at some time in the past; and just as one might find it rather strange to think of 'my French' as existing in 'inner space', it is precisely as strange to think of confidence or courage in this way.

The kinds of entity with which we tend to populate our 'inner worlds', whether personal qualities and strengths, weaknesses, 'personality traits' or 'symptoms' of 'psychopathology', are traceable to and perhaps most often understandable as the historical acquisitions or impositions of the proximally mediated influences on our lives. They may also be held in place by current environmental influences either of our particular personal circumstances or by cultural aspects of that part of the environment which forms a constituent of our personhood and which therefore we share with others – these latter aspects I shall return to presently.

A benign psychology would in my view (and no doubt often does, though not always sufficiently self-consciously) point out to people how much their own self-attributions of personal weakness and blame, of having interior flaws or moral failings, are actually the result of an ideological mystification which obscures an entirely exterior deprivation or exploitation. Where such deprivation or exploitation has taken place far enough in the past for its origin to be beyond the easy reach of memory, or indeed in that prelinguistic period of life in which memory cannot properly be said to be operating (and where events get 'remembered' only as indecipherable metaphors or unexplainable 'feelings'), then their manifestation in the present will often be, perhaps irresolvably, baffling. Sometimes, however, the nature of the ideologically distorted, inward projection of an outer deprivation is very obvious.

Among the more affluent sections of society it is not considered eccentric – it is not even considered a question of 'personality type' – to enjoy a degree of privacy in one's life. To have domestic space in which to live undisturbed by others, in a house set back from noisy roads, with a reasonably secluded garden enclosed by a suitably high hedge or wall, to own a car capable of transporting you quickly and privately behind its smoked-glass windows through the public space which separates your house from places of work or recreation – these are not considered the unusually quirky needs of somehow vulnerable personalities. Indeed, they are rarely considered as 'needs' at all (nothing so interior!) but rather the obviously valuable requisites of a normally comfortable life. We do not impute the 'need' for a hedge to any kind of neurotic personal deficit. And yet what happens to people when the opportunity to enjoy this kind of privacy is denied?

One thing that quite often happens is that they get diagnosed as 'agoraphobic'. Presumably those of us who enjoy privacy do so because we feel uncomfortable if exposed to the public gaze at times and in situations where we want to be 'off duty'. For people who *cannot* be off duty such discomfort may be almost perpetual. It is not, after all, uncommon for life to be lived (especially by women) in a house or flat constantly invaded by the sound, if not the sight, of others, set among hedgeless gardens (if any) and wall-less streets; for walks to the shops or bus stops to be exposed to the gaze of every idling youth, every casual mechanic working on his car, every curious consciousness possibly lurking behind every net curtain; for each bus that has to be taken itself to constitute a mobile aisle of inquisitive eyes. The screaming discomfort which such situations often engender is not 'diagnosed' as a lack of privacy to be 'cured' through the provision of an adequately constructed and tended physical environment, but is projected inward as 'agoraphobia' and 'treated' with drugs and psychotherapy.

Mrs Arkwright moved from a bleak public housing estate – open, asphalt, streaked with graffiti, litter and dog shit – where her existence anywhere beyond her own front door had been one of perpetual tension if not outright fear, to a new house she and her husband had bought in a pleasant residential suburb a few miles away. From the moment of her move her 'agoraphobia' started to diminish until after a few months it became most of the time absent from her awareness. At first, though, she was puzzled and mistrustful of herself, almost ashamed. 'Do you think there's something peculiar about me?' she asked soon after moving house. 'It sounds funny to say it, I know, but it's so nice to walk down roads lined with trees.' She was genuinely afraid that what she took to be a personal weakness before – feeling anxious when walking down 'dog muck lane' – had been replaced by another personal weakness in the form of a somehow reprehensible or abnormal sensitivity to landscape. When asked to think about *why* the trees had been planted in the streets of her new neighbourhood, she was lost for a clear answer; it was as if she could only think of them as having come to be there by accident.

The more negative, though nonetheless essential, task of a psychology which sets out to explode the myth of 'inferiority' is to point out that our strengths are no more to be held to our credit than our weaknesses are to our discredit. Whatever may make an individual admirable or effective as a human being does not arise from some unanalysable well of interior moral superiority, but, in all likelihood, from the good fortune of having had *imposed* upon him or her (for example, through the proximal influence of education) abilities and characteristics which become part of an embodied repertoire of resources.

That we almost always experience and talk about as inside those constituents of our personhood which are actually outside leads to profound confusion not only in our self-understanding, but also in our ideas about how to change ourselves and influence the environment. Such confusion is bound to follow on the radical mistake of supposing that social structures outside ourselves are actually moral or psychological structures inside ourselves. For then we either take upon ourselves or apportion to others the blame for faults or shortcomings which, in fact, lie outside us (and them), very probably in the world we share in common, and which can only be set right by attending to that world.

'FORM'

As social beings we live according to shared rules of meaning which are constructed to take account of, organize and explicate the immediate sense of the world (sensation) given to us by our bodies. Language is an example of one such set of rules – we cannot, in our shared experience of the world and our need to communicate intelligibly about it, step outside the linguistic rules which we have created for precisely this purpose. As I have indicated, though language forms an intensely personal and fundamentally important part of 'me', it is not 'inside' me, but exists in the social space I share with others.

Practically all the rules and concepts which give shape and meaning to our experience (many of them, of course, themselves constructed linguistically) are of this kind: they are not our personal inventions, but are acquired by us in the process of becoming *people*, i.e., as we interact bodily with the social environment which surrounds us. For the sake of brevity and quick reference I shall, with an apologetic nod to Plato, call such rules and concepts 'forms', not least because it is such rules and concepts which, precisely, give *form* to our experience. Without there being public forms which (nearly always) pre-exist our bodily experience of the world, resonate with and give meaning to it, we should live in a completely unintelligible, unarticulated and nondiscussable fog of confusion.

To take a very obvious example, but one nevertheless very important to our emotional wellbeing, one's sense of oneself as male or female is inseparable from the 'forms' of masculinity and femininity which are culturally established quite independently of us as individuals. To talk unreflectively of 'my' masculinity runs the risk of conceptualizing it as 'inside' me as some kind of personal possession. In fact, of course, how far I may be considered masculine or not depends upon a 'form' of masculinity which is entirely outside me. A great and often very damaging mistake is made when *a disintegration of the 'form' is interpreted or experienced as a breakdown in the individual personality.* Psychotherapy and clinical psychology, not to mention psychiatry, are the greatest perpetrators of this error, and in turning impersonal difficulties into personal problems have helped shape a culture of individualism where it has become almost impossible for people to differentiate inside from outside and to attribute the pain they so often feel about them-'selves' to its appropriate source.

Political movements are less likely to make this kind of error. Feminism, for example, in its political aspect, correctly sees that for women to gain a more equitable share of social power requires a change in the 'forms' relating to femininity and masculinity; feminists do not suggest (and insofar as they occasionally do they are mistaken) that each individual woman needs to change her 'self'. Psychological approaches to personal distress, on the other hand, are likely to fail to recognize that distress is often the pain of an individual who finds that he or she is unable to meet the requirements of 'form'. A person may, for example, be brought up in a field of proximal power which impresses a gender role of a certain kind, only to find that when he or she moves into a slightly more distal field of power (on escaping from the family, for example) there are new 'forms' of gender which make un-fulfillable, and perhaps even for the greater part unintelligible, demands (an extreme example would be a demand for homo- to be replaced by heterosexuality, or vice versa). The 'problem' here lies in the change in the outside world, not in some kind of personal inadequacy.

While psychologists no longer expect their clients to be able to alter their sexual proclivities at will, they still often assume that people do have access 'within' them to forms of conduct more appropriate or 'adjusted' than those they are currently displaying, and that all that is needed is some kind of (again, unanalysed) moral effort, perhaps inspired by a flash of 'emotional insight'. Apart from anything else, what is not recognized is the often very disturbing *unfamiliarity* which such a change of practice requires. In order to 'behave appropriately' the individual in such circumstances has to submit or be submitted to procedures of learning which nobody – least of all psychologists and therapists – understands and which require him or her to venture out into completely uncharted territory. 'Forms' are acquired bodily through the impress of power *from outside*. To acquire new 'forms' (i.e., to 'con-form' to new demands) when old ones have disappeared or disintegrated may or may not be possible, but in any case this is an issue about which 'therapies' and 'treatments' have had, so far, almost nothing useful to say.

Where an individual's experience cannot receive its meaning from an appropriate public form the result is likely to be experienced as either poetry or pain: the first a struggle to *create* form, the second the expression (or sensation) of its lack. There do exist, however, 'forms' for such pain itself, and those most usually invoked are blame and guilt. People who find themselves isolated with feelings, impulses, ideas or thoughts which find no ready echo in formal, public concepts or meanings are likely to succumb to a guilty sense of failure. They are also likely to find a psychiatric/therapeutic industry only too ready to produce a formal diagnosis for their difficulty.

Pam, suffering from 'depression', for which at times she has been variously 'treated' with electric shock and 'antidepressant' medication, at last finds the words with which to describe her predicament (though they do not, of course, solve it): 'It's as if I have feelings I don't know how to describe, because I was never told how to describe them. There were certain things we were just not allowed to be when we were little – there was no such thing as anger or hatred. I still don't really know what they are. I just know I have feelings, or I suppose they're feelings, which I don't know how to talk about. There's just a hole where I'm supposed to be feeling.' When in that hole, which happens quite often, Pam just sits helplessly with tears pouring down her cheeks. There is nothing really wrong *with* Pam. For one reason or another her parents failed to communicate some essential forms of feeling to her. They didn't (no doubt for the best of motives) want her to be hateful, so they never taught her how to hate, or what hatred was, and thus left her all alone with a feeling which is just a terrifying mystery to her, and about which the only communicable thing she *can* feel is guilt. But the failure, such as it is, is not and never was *inside* her. It was a failure of form. Failures of form may come about, as in Pam's case, through a failure of proximal powers to mediate them, or through the cultural absence or disintegration of forms capable of giving sense to individual experience. Our experience is unintelligible if we are not taught a language with which to describe it.

What makes some manifestations of 'psychopathology' so puzzling is precisely the fact that there are for one reason or another no adequate 'forms' through which they can be rendered socially intelligible. 'Madness' is not, as it is so often said to be, the person's 'loss of contact with reality', but rather reality's failure to make contact with and to explicate the personal experience of the sufferer. What makes somebody 'mad' is not some mysterious internal process or biological fault 'inside' him or her, nor indeed an internal breakdown of personal rationality, but the failure of outer form to give communicable meaning to his or her experience of a world which is and was precisely as real as any other. Though well recognized by some who have worked in this field (and explicated most profoundly and brilliantly in my view by H. S. Sullivan[3]), it seems extraordinarily difficult for this perspective on psychological distress and 'madness' to become sufficiently firmly established to develop productively. Over and over again the orthodox theoretical stance favours some kind or other of 'internal' pathology. It is as if horticulture had never progressed beyond a notion that the growth and health of plant life depended on the internal adjustment of each individual specimen rather than upon the conditions in which they grow.

'Psychopathology' can sometimes be rendered nonpathological through being given meaning by a 'form' not previously available. I have in this way once or twice seen how the conduct of someone supposedly suffering from an 'obsessional-compulsive neurosis' can become entirely appropriate if environmental influences shift in such a way as to accommodate it. For example, a man who worries more or less incessantly about whether he is accidentally

3. See his *The Interpersonal Theory of Psychiatry*, W. W. Norton, 1953.

transmitting a fatal disease to his nearest and dearest suddenly comes into his own (and becomes a lot happier) when he is given the job of safety officer where he works. It is rather as if he has suddenly found the role that life had in some mysterious way prepared him for.

Our private experience is, then, not only given meaning, but may also actually be rendered sane by finding shape in public form. My eccentricity may be like a key in search of a lock. It may, of course, never encounter one, in which case I may always feel isolated, sad or guilty. If, on the other hand, it *does* find one, I may become, perhaps joyfully, *associated* in a world which suddenly has a use for what I know.

The more systems of meaning, 'choices' of 'lifestyle' and moral conduct come to be seen as individual matters of 'personal responsibility', and so on, the more society becomes quite literally disintegrated. Social cohesion, shared meaning and purposive association become splintered into a mass of private idiosyncrasies, united paradoxically only by a common interest in self and structured by little other than market forces. Occasions designed ostensibly for communication or co-ordinated action (meetings and conferences, for example) become merely opportunities for the serial utterance of isolated views: all people share is a chance to speak out into a public space eerily devoid of receptivity, flat and without echo. To gain fleetingly a 'high profile', to be famous for fifteen minutes, to air your view, to flit momentarily across a television screen, is about the most use of public space one can ever hope to achieve. The radio phone-in which strings together a heterogeneous range of unrelated and totally inconsequential opinions provides a model of our shared world.

There is, in my view, little doubt that it is in the interest of the distal powers of a virtually global economy which depends on ceaseless growth, mediated more proximally by the complex disciplinary machinery of a managerial bureaucracy, to manufacture a mass consumership intent on its private satisfactions, trained to attribute its discomforts to 'internal' faults and failings, and detached from public 'forms' which might make possible an accurate critique of its situation. We are, however, entirely social creatures unable to live without common meanings (unless as a collectivity of mad people, which seems unlikely), and there are risks attached to exploitation on this scale.

There is a distinct danger that if 'form' disintegrates to the extent that the resulting famine of meaning becomes unbearable (as it might, for example, if our shared commitment to consumerism were frustrated by economic collapse) the fractured social collectivity would suddenly coalesce around 'forms' of a more sinister kind than those so far considered. By this I mean forms which are not so much social as biological, i.e., which are less the result of meaning through bodily *interaction* with the world than of our shared bodily structure alone. It does not seem implausible to suggest that a culture could become so impoverished of meaning (in respect of satisfactorily socially elaborated 'forms') that people would be thrown back simply on the demands and dictates of their physical needs and the basic, if not primitive, biological structures of sensation and emotion which fuel them.

Fright, anger, superstition and suspicion are prominent among the basic biological characteristics which we have in common, and it is surely no accident that when social cohesion can no longer be maintained through common allegiance to culturally sophisticated and highly developed categories of meaning, one witnesses the emergence of aggressive, magical and paranoid forms of social order – as for example in genocidal racialism, religious fanaticism and other forms of association round fundamentally irrational but emotionally highly charged systems of meaning. These do not stretch out in any attempt to engage with the complexities of a real environment, but rather reach back to cohere around the primitive physical engines of emotion which we all share – and *because* we all share them in such a basic way, such coherence can give rise to a sudden intensity which can be, as terribly destructive as it is, for those caught up in it, extraordinarily exhilarating.

CHAPTER FOUR

Case Study: The 1980s

The previous chapter attempts to sketch out a primarily theoretical account of the way in which the operation of social power may come to be reflected in individual experience – in particular the experience of distress. I hope that somewhat abstract discussion may have laid the ground for, and made more easily comprehensible, the concrete consideration to be offered in this chapter of how the processes involved may be played out in the actual events of a given time and place.

My central thesis is, of course, that individual, so-called 'psychopathology' cannot be understood out of the environmental context in which it occurs, and indeed cannot accurately be attributed to any pathological process *inside* people. It is, in fact, more correctly characterized as a pathology *of* the environment. One very obvious implication of this is that the 'symptoms' of 'pathology' will fluctuate and vary according to what is happening in the social environment, and it will not be possible scientifically to develop a system of classification which attempts to pin down for all time the nature of human psychological aberration. A purely biological approach, as, for example, in psychiatry, does attempt to do just that (and present-day efforts to arrive at a watertight classification of 'neurosis' and 'psychosis' are as energetically pursued within psychiatry as they were a hundred years ago). But variations in the expression of human distress are nowhere near as constant and reliably stable as are, say, the variations in botanical species which permit of the kind of classificatory system so envied by Kraepelin and his heirs.

The theoretical approach outlined in the previous chapter

makes it clear why this should be so: we do not so much have a relatively constant physical environment providing a home for a luxuriant variety of widely differing psychological specimens, but rather a highly unstable environmental context seething with often unspecifiable social influences in which people, at their core more or less identical biological atoms, are tossed and turned, shaped and constrained in an infinity of ways. When we, the atoms in this social cauldron, give vent to the pain its vicissitudes cause us, it is not because there is anything 'wrong' with our essential make-up, but because there are, or have been, things in our environment which would better not be there.

In seeking to understand these processes one may point, as I have attempted to do in the last chapter, to the relatively stable manner of their operation – the way, for example, in which proximal relations mediate distal influences – but one cannot give a lasting scientific description of their content, as this is constantly in flux. Psychiatrists and psychologists have at times paused to wonder over the fact that 'symptoms' of 'mental illness' change over different generations – that, for example, the 'hysterical' blindnesses and paralyses which apparently afflicted so many people a century or so ago have now virtually disappeared – but they have not fully absorbed the significance of this phenomenon. It is not that the nature of personal pathology has undergone some kind of mutation, nor that such 'symptoms' are not somehow 'real', but that changes have taken place in the kinds of social influences which bear down upon us.

One cannot, then, hope to say anything eternally true about the actual phenomena of our distress, the content of our pain. We can only fight a kind of running battle to keep track of it. For this reason, in trying to put flesh on the theoretical bones mainly considered so far, I shall take as 'clinical material' not a range of exemplary 'cases' intended to stand for all time as typical instances of 'disease', but a *decade* – the 1980s – identifiable, I believe, for a set of social-environmental influences which mark it out from those immediately preceding it (though not perhaps so distinctly from other decades earlier in this and in the last century). Because of the relativity of social space-time, I also have to limit my case study to a place – Britain. How far the observations to follow have relevance to other times and places I must leave it to others to judge, and whether the 1990s will be significantly different from the 1980s must also remain to be seen.

The fact that it is most essentially the environment which is the source of our troubles does not mean that it does not affect us, at distinct points of space and time, in ways which have a certain discernible regularity. While men and women in distress should not, for the reasons I have given, be categorized as instantiating 'psychopathology', they may nevertheless show recognizable similarities as being victims of a similar fate. In this way 1980s Britain can be approached from two aspects which I shall consider here separately: the environment itself, and its principal effects on the people who inhabit it (the characters it affects).

I   THE ENVIRONMENT

There are people far more able and qualified than I to give an account of the wider sociological perspective on how 'postmodern' culture, politics and economics burst upon Britain towards the end of the 1970s (see, for example, David Harvey's admirable *The Condition of Postmodernity*). Much of the more limited perspective that I can offer has been gained through the eyes – not to mention the sensibilities and pain – of the characters who provide the models for the second part of this chapter. From their proximal struggles with a world which most of them saw as the creation of their own inadequacy, I have, I think, been able to discern the operation of more distal influences giving rise to a common culture.

The furthest that reflective people who have lived through this decade were likely to see as they tried to make out the shapes of influence at the edge of their power horizon was the silhouette of Margaret Thatcher and her entourage of apparently unusually ruthless and determined enthusiasts for economic liberalism, the results of the abolition of 'welfarism' and 'socialism', and the restructuring of Britain according to a philosophy of self-reliance and the relentless pursuit of personal interest. However, even the most cursory glance at the literature of social criticism stemming from the USA – or even merely superficial attention to events in the American political arena – quickly lengthens the perspective.

Margaret Thatcher and her government were merely representatives of a culture which had been flourishing in the Western world long before it made its presence so forcibly felt in Britain. The political influence was not the origin of this culture, but the concentration of power which gave it impetus. The Thatcher government were not the originators but the engineers – the managers – of powers which had already thoroughly dominated the other side of the North Atlantic for some time, and were now blowing across it in a gale. Indeed, what brought Thatcher's downfall just after the close of the decade was not her failure as a politician but her failure as a manager. She was too much of an individualist, and had become an obstacle rather than an enabler of the powers whose path she had up till then done so much to smooth. She was replaced by a man who was barely a politician at all in the sense of having a personal vision or a passionate commitment to an ideal of societal organization – he was quintessentially General Manager (UK).

It is extremely difficult even for the reasonably well-educated, well-informed person possessed of access to some of the more distal powers which social advantage confers to penetrate the murky depths of power which the politics of Western democracies screen. All one can tell with any certainty is that economic conglomerates whose power cannot even accurately be measured (if only because they operate beyond the boundaries of any one authority competent to do the measuring) set in motion interests which are fertilized and nourished by the social conditions in which they take root.

Huge cross-national companies dependent for their survival on ever-increasing expansion float round the global market like giant economic icebergs, crashing into and fusing with each other, while the waves they make are absorbed, and eventually controlled and directed by armies of producers, consumers and enablers (managers) who will typically be located in those parts of the world best designed for their function.

The processes of production and the kinds of alienation and exploitation they involve – and which so preoccupied sociologists and political economists of the last half of the nineteenth century and the first half of this – have to a great extent drifted out of the sight of the citizens of affluent Western nations. This is, of course, by no means because they have ceased to exist, but because they have been exported to parts of the globe where labour can be bought more cheaply and conditions of production controlled less scrupulously. While so far as Britain is concerned this has had little visible effect on the ideology of class, it has certainly made some difference to the actual class structure. People ideologically labelled 'working class' became during the eighties far less likely than formerly to be members of an organized, self-consciously unionized industrial workforce, and were, in fact, either likely not to be working at all (becoming part of an 'underclass' existing outside the formal economic structure) or to be engaged in some form of industrially unproductive work, quite possibly in a role to be seen as to an extent 'upwardly mobile'. There was also on the labour market a steadily increasing number of people who had gained formal qualifications in subjects (social sciences, business and media studies, etc.) which led them to expect employment in some form of managerial or other 'white collar' capacity.

The population of countries such as Britain thus became more preoccupied either with the business of consumption, from the point of view both of fulfilling the unwritten duties of consumer and of maximizing the opportunities for others to do so (swelling the ranks of the 'service industries'), or with mediating the complex social powers which the global as well as national economies demanded. While these two roles – those of consumer on the one hand and mediator on the other – can be separated from each other only with a degree of artificiality, I shall for the sake of clarity consider them here one at a time.

The Mediators

The impress of distal power shapes and engages with the interests already structuring social organization in such a way as to carry through its projects with the minimum of resistance. The social revolution which took place almost anonymously in Britain in the eighties took advantage of the proximal needs, aspirations and self-perceptions of a relatively (in global terms) affluent and well-educated populace in order to render the country as a whole far more responsive than it had been to the imperatives of big business. To move money quickly and easily, to dissolve obstacles in the way of rationalization of working practices, and, perhaps most essentially, to expand the scope and influence of the market, meant the wholesale and ruthless removal of as much as possible of the pre-existing social institutions and ideology identifiable as incompatible with these aims. This was to be the Business Revolution, and in order to achieve its aims not only would existing business people be enthusiastically recruited to the cause, but nonbusiness people would have to be – sometimes, but in fact surprisingly seldom, more reluctantly – re-shaped and retrained into *becoming* business people.

A significant part of the ideology of 'postmodernism' or 'postindustrialism' was designed to loosen allegiance to 'outmoded' intellectual, philosophical and ethical systems which threatened to impede the permeation of every level of society by business concepts and practices. The bluntly calculating language of accountancy – the 'bottom line' of costs and benefits – had first to oust and then to take over the function of 'old' concepts such as 'goodness' and 'truth'. There can, I submit, be almost nobody reading these pages who was not in some way or other during the eighties caught up in or affected by the extraordinary upheavals which attended the ideological as well as the more crudely material triumphs of the revolution. To some extent or other we all helped to mediate these processes; we had no choice.

To replace with the values of the market, within the space of a decade, the ideology of a social system which at least purported to be based on the values of truth, justice and equality traceable back to the Enlightenment was no mean achievement. Its accomplishment demanded three main thrusts:

1. The application of raw (coercive and economic) power at the distal region of the political system. Here Mrs Thatcher obliged with a ruthlessness scarcely experienced in the memory of postwar generations. The breaking of the unions following the repression of the miners, the remorseless 'rationalization' of heavy industry and the engineering of mass unemployment, the dismantling of the structures of welfare and protection for the poor and the weak, and the deregulation of any system which offered either economic or intellectual privilege of any kind (for example protection against economic competition; professional freedom of self-determination), set in motion the conditions for a radical insecurity more than sufficient to induce the co-operation of the entire population in realization of the aims of the brave new business world.

Since my central aim is to explicate the way distal power becomes mediated proximally as psychological or emotional distress, I shall not consider its origins and dynamics in any greater detail here. This should not, however, lead us to ignore its enormous importance; without the application of such distal power the following discussion would have been neither necessary nor possible.

2. The construction of a high-level, articulate and defensible intellectual rationale. It is here that we encounter the intelligentsia of 'postmodernity'. I must admit that I find it difficult to discern the nature and significance of the role of those who managed to lay the foundations of a superordinate philosophy which

scornfully swept aside the Enlightenment values we have supposedly misled ourselves with for the past two hundred years. I would not for a moment suggest that those who attacked our, apparently, pathetic notions of abiding truth (Richard Rorty), reality and objectivity (François Lyotard), or individual integrity in thought and idea (Jacques Derrida), somehow colluded with distal powers to become apologists for their aims. Nor, to tell the truth, am I sure how much their activities really mattered, especially as part of the achievement of the Business Revolution was to discredit and dilute the value and power of intellectual activity itself. However this may be, the result of the new pragmatism was to help remove from the ideological pipeline any awkward little lumps or bumps likely to prove resistant to the smooth flow of endlessly recyclable, critically unstoppable, always expansible market rhetoric. A world without truth is an adman's dream, and, when it comes to respect for truth, there was left following the revolution almost no distinction between the most exalted strata of the academy and the most banal fabrications of television advertising.

In large part, I suspect, the intellectual respectability which 'postmodernism', 'deconstruction' and so on, gave, perhaps unwittingly, to the operation of the market was generated by the influence upon Academe of the market itself. Under market pressures, 'truth' either becomes diluted into the endlessly multipliable uncritical jargons of a half-educated mediocracy (see below), or else it becomes impacted and squeezed into the fearsome locutions of those superintelligent, hypererudite academics who, to succeed in a university knowledge industry where there is simply not enough truth to go around, must spin ever more ingenious and rarefied critical visions out of a strictly limited stock of basic themes. Hence, for example, the popularity among literary theorists of the speculations of psychoanalysis or 'poststructuralism' which, respectively, suggest that meanings are not what they appear to be, and that ideas are not attributable in any significant sense to the people who had them. It is not so much that such conceptions are necessarily wrong or intellectually valueless, but that, to sustain and elaborate the academic market, good faith is likely to give way to the cultivation of novelty. Intellectual debate at the highest level becomes but a high-flown variation on the 'new blue whitener' theme invented to boost the flagging sales of an already perfectly adequate detergent.

The upshot of all this, anyway, was that during the eighties the academy became no longer the refuge of disinterested seekers after truth, nor somewhere to go in search of resistance to Business values. This may, in fact, have been a much more serious loss than might be suggested by the rather equivocal position occupied by intellectuals in the power structure of the Business Revolution. It seems probable that part of the, perhaps unconscious, appeal to many people of the revolution itself was its irreverence towards various kinds of 'professionals' – not least university teachers – who had formerly been able to take advantage of a deferential respect they undoubtedly (because they are human) did not always earn. Whatever the occasional pomposity and impracticality of their occupants, however, the universities had nevertheless been the guardians of some of the most central and essential 'forms' of post–Enlightenment society. The dilution of the concept of truth and the redefinition of knowledge as a ready-made commodity in which people may be trained (rather than as something to be *discovered* by people who have the ability, the time and the necessary patronage to look for it) threatened to make higher learning into a mere extension of shop-floor instruction and to remove from it the possibility of developing any kind of critique of the business culture.

Business must dispense with truth if it is to avoid limits on its expansion and to be able ceaselessly to invent new needs. It has, indeed, a concept ready made to slip into the place of truth – fashion – which far more adequately suits its books. It can, furthermore, happily substitute training for the pursuit of knowledge since its aim is a) to maintain a technology of management by managers who do not reflect upon their role, and b) to instruct a mass consumership in the technology of consumption. It will, it is true, need to preserve an essentially scientific/technological élite in Research and Development, but it has no use for the humanities except as markets. It will also prefer oblivion to history, since fashion can be recycled more quickly if everything seems 'new'. All in all Business can do without higher education, and if given half a chance, as the 1980s demonstrated, will do.

3. The installation of a social apparatus of proximal mediation: i.e., of those whose task it was to convey the influence of the distal 'revolutionary' powers to men and women in the street. In order to slide into place anything so one-track minded and ethically and intellectually impoverished as the Business Culture, there are required towards the practical and ideological base of the social pyramid multitudes of willing workers. It would be utter madness to suppose that revolutions such as these are achieved through the connivance of a vast officialdom in the *conscious* exploitation of the mass of the citizenry. What is needed, rather, is the enthusiastic co-operation of well-meaning – even altruistic – people in a project they are fully able to believe in. Once someone is convinced that his or her 'motives' are of the best, he or she can be happily recruited to literally any kind of cause (it may be paradoxical but it certainly isn't even improbable that concentration camp guards really *could* be nice people).

The explanation for the paradox – for the involvement, that is, of benign people in malign activities – is, of course, to be found in our mistaken attribution of the reasons for things to the interior motives and impulses of the people who enact them. As far as the Business Revolution was concerned, there were at the end of the seventies armies of people whose best intentions could easily be invoked as their various interests were engaged in the revolutionary cause. Many of these people already formed part of the business world; others, products of an expanded tertiary education system, were massing at the boundaries of established professional territory, not quite possessing the élite credentials for entry, but close enough to be convinced that given a chance they could do at least as good a job. Self-confident, eager for opportunity, ready to serve and poised for what could only be seen as a thoroughly deserved slice of upward mobility, this vast class of mediators suddenly found itself, once the gates of the established social institutions and professions gave way, rushing into the positions which were waiting for it. The rule of the mediocracy had begun.

A Business society built solely on the imperatives of economic rationality and consumerism could not be run by a hypocritical cadre composed of people consciously compromising the 'old' values of goodness, truth and justice. It had rather to make use of people only half instructed in the traditional culture, sufficiently blissful in their ignorance to install the simple-minded precepts and practices of monetarism and the 'classless society' with absolute conviction. Attachment to knowledge, scholarship, ethical reflection and analysis, logical or epistemological scrupulosity, was a definite impediment to the Business world, and those foolish enough not to relinquish such attachments voluntarily were likely to find themselves the objects of intensive training courses which, whatever the 'package' of 'skills' they pretended to impart, were really forms of instruction in the financial, commercial and promotional languages of Business.

Business language, Business mores, Business fashions and 'lifestyles' surged during the eighties into every stratum of British social life. University lecturers found themselves abandoning corduroys and pullovers for smart dark suits and flowery ties; previously anonymous clerks and typists turned, overnight it seemed, into the power-dressed houris of the television series *Dallas*. Doctors found themselves studying business systems rather than case histories; teachers became preoccupied less with lessons than with 'income generation'.

To those who enjoyed their new activities, perhaps their participation seemed like an act of personal choice – certainly many seemed to embrace the new culture as if they'd been waiting for it all their lives. To many others, however, the new era dawned as in a dream, an almost-nightmare in which they donned their shoulder-padded jackets and forced their ethical conceptions into the ledgers of accountancy with a sense of stunned unreality: they seemed to *want* to do these things (else why would they be doing them?) but felt nevertheless painfully out of tune with themselves. Yet others found themselves unable to cope with the demands of daily life and looked around for help.

Most interesting of all, almost nobody seemed aware that the world had radically changed and that a revolution had taken place. It was just life, from day to day. This does not mean that the revolution was achieved without anguish. Bloodless it may have been. Largely unremarked upon it certainly was by the vast majority whose view extended little further than the ambit of their own domestic lives. But it was certainly not achieved without cost in terms of distress and personal disintegration.

The composition of the 'mediocracy' closely reflected the principal concerns of the culture. Alasdair MacIntyre[1] wrote compellingly right at the beginning of the decade on the significance of managers and therapists to a social world which had abandoned virtue, and Robert Bellah et al.[2] again highlighted the role of these two groups in maintaining what they call the utilitarian individualism of American culture. Certainly management on the one hand and therapy and 'counselling' on the other are among the most prominent components of modern mediocracies. One should also note the important ideological role of the advertising and promotional industry, as well as the essential disciplinary function of what Christopher Lasch[3] has called the 'tutelary complex': those whose job it is to set and maintain the normative standards of society, including counsellors and trainers of various kinds and extending deep into the fields of education

1. See his *After Virtue*, 2nd ed., Duckworth, 1985.
2. *Habits of the Heart*, Hutchinson, 1988.
3. *The Minimal Self. Psychic Survival in Troubled Times*, Pan Books, 1985.

and social work. All such people stand between the individual and the world in order to mediate his or her experience of it in accordance with the aims of a Business Culture. For the most part these aims are twofold: to establish the ideology of the culture and to extend the market.

MANAGEMENT

The 'manager's right to manage' was a prominent slogan of the early part of the decade, and certainly the managers' role in forcing into place the disciplinary and instructional apparatus of the revolution was crucial to its success. Traditional methods of assessing vocational ability and professional competence, embedded institutional practices of hiring and firing, long accepted (even if unspoken and unwritten) rules concerning the rights and duties of employers and employed were suddenly replaced by new definitions of competence, formal systems of appraisal, restrictions on information and communication, and authoritarian lines of accountability. These 'new' systems of discipline and surveillance, backed by the very real threat of unemployment, were usually introduced as the spin-off of reorganization and change, and extended across the entire working world forms of uncertainty and insecurity which had previously been the lot only of an exploited industrial workforce.

Virtually no place of work escaped the upheavals of reorganization: large public institutions in health and education, small family businesses, public and private companies of every size and description seemed to be overrun by management consultants advising on change and trainers instructing in its accomplishment. The besuited managerial group having a 'time out' weekend at an expensive country club could equally well turn out to be the board of a large engineering firm, a group of NHS administrators, or the senior academic staff of a university department. Everyone who wasn't made redundant underwent a change of role or a change of rank, everyone was taught the new language of efficiency and effectiveness, quality control, appraisal and time management. Everyone, no matter who or what, was sent on a course. I met a telephone engineer in a Dublin guesthouse who was just completing a five-day course on 'the management of change' – he was, he said with a wonderfully ironic smile, due to take his retirement in six weeks' time.

If the aim of this managed upheaval in the lives of almost everyone was intended to realize the claims of its superficial rhetoric – that 'time' could be 'managed', for example – it could only be considered a disastrous failure, for the most likely sequel to 'training days' was organizational chaos. If, on the other hand, its actual achievements – of disconcerting, disorientating, and rendering the workforce receptive through sheer vulnerability to the new business ideology – if these were its real intentions, then it was an immense success. The sublime confidence with which the managerial mediocracy imposed its debased language of 'performance indicators', 'Total Quality', and so on, on people who had all their lives spoken, albeit uncritically, a far more ethically nuanced language left them conceptually completely off balance.

The captives of the mediocracy thus struggled (often with surprising good will and docility) to force the previously unarticulated complexity of their experience into the linguistic moulds imposed by the hyped-up banalities of Businessese. To a puzzling extent they seemed unaware that rather than being offered a 'whole new way' of 'developing their management skills', or whatever, they were in fact being robbed of the linguistic tools to express the violence being done to their understanding. Their docility – indeed their often apparently eager compliance – in this process is, however, only puzzling if one forgets that people judge intention on the basis of proximal relations, not distal objectives. Managerial mediocrats are often very nice people, completely unaware of the sources of the power they are mediating, and it's hard to take exception to their activity if you locate the reasons for it somewhere behind their kind and obviously well-meaning eyes.

The mediocracy maintains the credibility of its managerial rule, as well as the ultimate viability of its enterprise, by exploiting the knowledgeable. It cannot, of course, become knowledgeable itself without ceasing to be mediocre. The exploitation of knowledge is achieved in two main ways. The first is through the importation into the business enterprise of outside consultants; the second is through the direct exploitation of 'inhouse' technical or professional knowledge.

The explosion in the use of management consultancy and training organizations during the eighties was at first sight hard to understand, not least as their employment seemed to run counter to the expressed management aim of cost-cutting. One thing that systems consultants, advisers on information technology and trainers in all kinds of personnel management functions were not was cheap. However, a closer examination of the relations between mediocratic managers and their consultant advisers reveals some interesting ideological gains for the former. In fact, technical consultancy was one of the principal tools through which the mediocracy could maintain managerial control without disclosure of its own ignorance. Technical and professional knowledge becomes 'mystified' as something which no manager could be *expected* to have, but which needs to be subject to management control through the exercise of economic power. Managerial 'expertise' thus becomes quite detached from technical know-how, which it makes economically subordinate – its servant rather than a necessary requirement of its own function. Not only, then, is mediocratic management protected from recognition of its own mediocrity, but it places itself in a relation of control over the technical knowledge which might otherwise threaten it. Business, in other words, can take over professional knowledge without having to go to the trouble of actually acquiring it.

One of my reasons for dwelling on this phenomenon is because of the 'pathology' it gave rise to in the eighties. Among the casualties of the working environment were to be found competent and successful professional and technical employees of both public and private concerns who had previously scarcely been represented at all in the typical clientele of clinical psychology. People who had formerly occupied positions of respect and influence suddenly found themselves sidelined by a mediocracy which first usurped their managerial function and then maintained its position by importing (at enormous, and what appeared to be unnecessary, expense) hired 'experts' to perform the very same technical/professional functions, but on its own terms. Even where professional expertise was not subjugated through the device of consultancy, many people performing technical functions vital to the concerns of an organization but incomprehensible to the mediocracy managing it found themselves in a painfully ambiguous role of indispensability coupled with low status. In the second part of this chapter I shall introduce one or two of the characters typical of this newly exploited class.

It should, of course, be absolutely no surprise that the management of a 'reality' which must be opened up fully to the dictates of the market would ally itself to a propaganda machine. Business and advertising naturally belong together. What was perhaps surprising in the eighties was the extent to which promotional ideology infiltrated its methods and its language into every corner of the culture. The first coup was indeed the redefinition of reality itself. A 'real world' was defined as one in which the ruthless relations of the market reigned supreme. This was the world where nothing was for nothing and the weak went to the wall. Any world constructed on alternative ethical lines was stamped as outmoded, deranged or dangerous. The 'real world' was a hard, cold world of self-made success, virulent moralism, uncompromising individualism and pitiless contempt for sociality of more or less any kind. Having thus defined the world it wished to colonize, Business culture left it to the mediocratic promotional machinery to package it seductively and fill in the ideological details, and suddenly the language was full of market hype.

Not only were social issues and problems of every kind approached through the 'attitude change' mythology of advertising – everything from the training of the unemployed to the fight against AIDS – but even the most sober representatives of high culture found themselves declaiming the virtues of their wares in the manically urgent language of the supermarket. Works of art, scientific theories, affairs of state, medical treatments, courses of higher education, would all be 'sold' with the same tired combinations of fatuous hyperbole. Everything was major, new (usually 'major-new' as a kind of compound attraction), unique, massive, important, 'important-new' and exciting. 'Stunning' and 'awesome' appeared a little later. Mediocrity was clothed as 'excellence'. Scarcely any social or vocational practice or pastime could be envisaged which did not seem both designed and expected to engender a kind of frantic excitement; the prescribed mode of mediocratic life was one of the mediation and consumption of euphoria, and anyone who attempted to engage in any other kind of activity, or speak a milder or more considered language, stood in danger of finding him or herself beyond the boundaries of the real world.

The Orwellian irony of 'the real world' is particularly poignant in the light of the promotional impetus of the eighties towards make-believe. For while on the one hand it was a 'real world' of economic rationality and throat-cutting competition, on the other it was one of wildly proliferating market diversification which had to be promoted and stoked by multimedia propaganda. Everything from the political manipulation of demographic statistics to the spells and potions of the 'alternative health' industry was aimed at making people believe not only that the harsh consequences of economic exploitation didn't really hurt, but that the world was positively bursting with opportunity and choice.

Make-believe also performed the job of disguising the inevitable results of emptying the public purse into private pockets. As public assets were stripped and public services depleted of the personnel necessary to run them safely and efficiently, curiously transparent attempts were made to paper over the all too obvious cracks. Examples that spring to mind are the VDUs that appeared in railway stations giving arrival and departure times of trains the spuriousness of which only became apparent to the infuriated traveller after he or she had been wildly misled a couple of times. 'Visitors' Centres' would issue hopeful tourists with 'information' on local events and transportation seemingly inspired by simple fantasy. Anybody who, however well-intentioned, could make money out of an expanding market in promises and appearances did. Prominent among the practitioners of make-believe were also, of course, the therapists and counsellors.

THERAPY AND COUNSELLING

If managers can be seen as the Machiavellian mediators of a disciplinary insecurity which provided the basis for Business Culture, therapists and counsellors were foremost among its gullibly well-intentioned ideologues. This might in some ways be unfair to managers. Though some certainly were, and prided themselves on being, Machiavellian – their role models the unscrupulous manipulators of *Dallas* – most were probably convinced that they were performing a necessary and socially useful task. In the case of therapists and counsellors there can be little doubt that very nearly without exception they were utterly certain that their profession was solely concerned with the humane relief of suffering, and if 'sincerity' (that typically 'internal' eighties substitute for external reality and truth) could be taken as a valid index of social role, then the activities of counselling and therapy would indeed have to be acknowledged as above reproach. I have met hundreds of psychotherapists and counsellors of many kinds from all sorts of professional, semiprofessional and amateur backgrounds, and I cannot think of one I would accuse of conscious charlatanism. They provide, in fact, a marvellous example of the way our motives can remain pure while our interests are engaged in the pursuance of enterprises of which we are completely unaware.

It is very easy to come to believe that one has a special gift for counselling. 'I'm a good listener'; 'People seem to find it easy to tell me their troubles'; 'X said it was the first time she'd ever told anybody about that': these are the kinds of experience which set many of us on the road to becoming counsellors. Because we observe the pleasure and relief with which people react to our listening attentively to their troubles, we feel we have discovered within ourselves some special gift of healing. In truth, however, such is likely to be the experience of *anyone* of reasonable intelligence and good will who can shut up long enough to allow someone else to talk. What we take to be a personal prerequisite for our vocation is merely a universal human potentiality. What it does do, however, is provide us with the inner conviction we need to embark upon a career in which we may with the highest moral probity profit from the distress of others. (At this point I think I sense some rising gorges among my readership. Let me therefore emphasize as strongly as I can that I am *not* denying all validity, moral or scientific, to counselling and psychotherapy. I shall be considering their positive potential in the next chapter.)

We must distinguish, then, between the well-meaning but ingenuous beliefs of therapists themselves about the significance of their role, and their actual functions as part of the mediocracy. The first such function is precisely that of appropriating and marketing aspects of care and concern which should constitute a part of the everyday ethical life of any humane society. In the developed Western world there are likely to be very few people who perceive any incongruity in the professional provision of sympathetic listening, and indeed there may well be an enduring social necessity for the kind of dispassionate confessional role formerly more the province of priests. With psychotherapy, however, this role becomes specifically commercialized, and we are made most acutely aware of this when it comes to the opening up of new markets.

During the eighties there was a positive explosion in the expansion of the therapy and counselling industry in Britain. The deregulation of the health care market allowed professional groups, voluntary workers and a wide range of the 'brand name' schools of psychotherapy and counselling to gain access to 'treatment' which had previously been the preserve of medicine and one or two of its satellite professions. As part of this process the market was extended in several new directions, and 'counselling' – previously considered a minority practice of doubtful validity – suddenly became the self-evidently necessary antidote to occasions of distress which up till then people had just had to muddle through as best they could. A particularly good example of this extension of the frontiers of the market into the previously noncommercial territory of ordinary social intercourse was that of 'disaster counselling' and the development of the concept of 'post-traumatic stress disorder'.

The need for the provision of aid and comfort to those involved – victims and their families, professional rescue workers – in 'major incidents' such as transport accidents and sports stadium disasters can scarcely be seen as a matter for debate. What may be questioned, however, is *how* such aid and comfort may best be achieved, and what was remarkable during the decade under consideration was the entirely uncritical way in which the prevailing winds of Business swept aside the traditional 'coping mechanisms' of family, neighbourhood and Church to put forward as the most obviously proper response a professional network of counselling.

As the letter pages of many a professional journal testified, therapists and counsellors disputed heatedly each others' qualifications to attend the scene and advise on the aftermath of such events, while commercial groups rapidly formed to lay claim to special expertise. A whole literature concerning the particular psychological characteristics and consequences of disasters sprang into existence practically overnight, research grants were applied for, and treatment programmes hastily constructed and advocated for anyone who could conceivably be counted as a victim (even down to people who had been disturbed by witnessing events on the television). Not one of those professionally involved in this activity, I am perfectly ready to be persuaded, had in their heart anything but sympathetic pain for the injured and bereaved, and an ardent wish to help. But equally few, it seemed, stopped to consider that by their very activity – by standing between individuals and the world to mediate their pain and grief – they were a) claiming for Business a previously noncommercial social function, and b) offering a service for the effectiveness of which there was no particularly convincing evidence.

A social services pamphlet issued in response to an aircraft disaster defined 'normal feelings' likely to be experienced by relatives or friends of victims, for example: 'fear of "breaking down" or "losing control" ', 'guilt for being better off than others, i.e., being alive, not injured . . .' It outlined likely physical and mental sensations, for example: 'Privacy – in order to deal with feelings, you will find it necessary at times to be alone, or just with family and close friends.' It offered some practical 'dos and don'ts', for example 'DON'T bottle up feelings. DO express your emotions and let your children share in grief', and gave guidance on when to seek professional help, for example: 'If after a month you continue to feel numb and empty.'

Now my point is not that such advice is wrong or misguided – much of it indeed is obvious common sense – but that it breaks down public 'forms' of appropriate social conduct and offers them back to the individual reconstituted as commercially available professional knowledge. Unintentionally, of course, it alienates people from their own bodily sensations and mediates their experience by making its meaning dependent on professional interpretation. The person becomes unable to say to him or herself: 'This terrible experience has numbed me', but must say rather: 'What can this strange numbness mean? I must seek the explanation from an appropriately qualified expert.' Once the need (in this case for 'counselling') has been created, the consumership then establishes a demand. No longer confident in their ability to handle their own distress as part of a traditional social process, people demand the presence of counsellors as a right.

There may be readers who find my argument far-fetched. It is obviously helpful, they might say, for people in such dreadful circumstances to have available professional reassurance and help: that cannot be taken as an indication of some commercial conspiracy to rob them of an understanding of their own feelings. To this I would respond that of course I imply no conspiracy – conspiracy is far too 'proximal' an activity to account for the kind of process I am trying to clarify. What I can say, on the other hand, is that in my role as clinical psychologist I am daily confronted with people who depend on me to read the significance of their own feelings, and it must in some sense be in the interests of professions such as mine to increase their number.

It was not only an expanding market in the mediation of experience which therapists were able to take advantage of in the eighties. There was also a marked increase in the possibilities for mediating relationship. The somewhat staid Marriage Guidance Council transformed its 'image', renamed itself 'Relate', extended its sphere of operations and became altogether a much more businesslike organization. (Whatever your 'business' in the eighties, it was *de rigueur* to refurbish your image and adopt a new logo.) Marital counsellors, sex therapists and dating agencies became the respectable end of a market whose business was procuring, in one way or another, emotional and sexual 'fulfilment'.

'Relationships' had, in fact, to bear a heavier and heavier strain as they became billed as the main source of warmth, intimacy and satisfaction in a world which was otherwise more coldly competitive than it had been for decades (I have written about this at some length in my book *Taking Care*). It was, then, not surprising to find a growing army of professional advisers at hand to counsel those who found the strain too great and, once again, to imply thereby that the business of relationship was no amateur matter. Relations between parents and children received similar attention – the decade which 'discovered' child sex abuse, and set up around it an extensive network of professional surveillance and correction, also constructed programmes and packages of 'parenting skills' which could be bought off the peg.

The function (as opposed to the conscious intention) of this mediocratic caste of therapists and counsellors was not only concerned with expanding the market for mediation of experience and relationship. It also provided shock-absorption for a society in which emotional and psychological, as well as physical, damage was a necessary part of its economic and ideological policies. Unemployment, ceaseless radical change, diminished status and insecurity all took their toll in the workplace and strained the domestic relations of people whose only recourse was 'counselling'. Counsellors performed the ideological function of representing as proximal causes of distress which were in fact distal, and then offered comfort and advice to those who identified themselves as falling short of the norm in 'coping skills', the 'management of stress', etc. What was essentially distal economic coercion was represented proximally as a remediable personal failure, and counsellors occupied the space vacated by reason in this conjuring trick to create a substitute 'credibility'.

The bridge over the credibility gap was at times exposed as a rhetoric too obviously shaky for anyone to trust – for example the suggestion that lack of a job reflected merely the unwillingness to look for one – but more often it was held in place through a suspension of rationality which could be maintained only by a curious kind of sentimentality. Personnel managers of large firms instituting programmes of redundancy could, for example, seriously set up as a humane measure the provision of counselling to those affected. An insult added to an injury was thus presented – and surprisingly often accepted – as a 'package of care' for which the redundant employee should feel grateful.

An aspect of their role from which nearly all counsellors are able (via the mystified notion of 'motivation') to dissociate themselves is thus one of increasing the likelihood of the very social evils whose effects they are supposedly there to mitigate. They do, certainly, offer forms of comfort which are often gratefully received by those in distress (the shock-absorbing function), but they also, through an ideology of personal change which suggests that people have a choice over their predicaments, make the occurrence of such predicaments more probable. Just as the 'redundancy counsellor' legitimizes putting people out of work, so the 'debt counsellor' makes more likely the irresponsible extension of credit, and the 'disaster counsellor' renders more conceivable the operation of a 'risk economics' (another phenomenon of the eighties) which calculates the 'acceptable' limits of expenditure on safety.

The Consumers – Markets on Life's Way

Consumerism is, of course, not just a phenomenon of the eighties, but the necessary ideology of an economic system which depends for its survival on limitless expansion of the market. The logic of this system, its adamantine rationality, is inexorable, and its triumphant progress has spanned much more than a mere decade, but the special contribution of the eighties was perhaps to slacken the few remaining ethical brakes on the raw injunction to consume which lies at the root of, at least, affluent Western societies.

Even if the shreds of alternative ways of life remaining from religious and political systems which had placed convivial sociality higher than economic self-interest constituted by the beginning of the decade little more than a kind of desperate hypocrisy, they were in any case swept away by the assertions of a 'new right' which proclaimed its philosophy of competitive individualism with absolute confidence. There was, said Mrs Thatcher, no such thing as society. For individuals and families to grab what they could for themselves was presented, and widely accepted, no longer as selfishness or greed, but merely as the obvious and inevitable

– and in a sense therefore the most sensible and virtuous – thing to do.

In this way the 'forms' which (again, even if crumbling) had been held in place by traditional institutions of ethical guidance became openly discredited, and in their place were enshrined the values authorized by Business. Parallel with a stern new morality of cost-effectiveness and rigorous competition there grew up a kind of redeeming therapeutics aimed at the rehabilitation of greed. Counselling became available for people who felt inhibited about money, for example, sufferers might be encouraged to gaze lovingly at a ten-pound note, expressing their desire for and appreciation of it in a therapeutic group of others similarly afflicted. Life had for most people long been structured and shaped by the need for money and the craving for consumer goods. So far as Britain was concerned, the eighties simply made such concerns official and provided a formal ideological framework in which they could flourish.

The most important social function of the vast majority of the population of a country such as Britain is to consume. It is true, of course, that so far our lives as social beings are ordered, perhaps even fundamentally, by public 'forms' of morality which arise more from our common humanity than from the dictates of consumerism, but such 'forms' have become tacit, unofficial, and survive only as the embodied practice of a collectivity of *individuals* who no longer have access to any coherent, clearly articulated, statement of them. The only values which are made manifest to someone living an everyday life are Business values.

During the eighties we became a monoculture in which just about every conceivable form of activity was appropriated by Business. Whatever was itself not business was sponsored by Business. The very language was adjusted in such a way as to strip people of any role other than that of being clients of Business. At various junctures, for example, both 'passengers' (on the railway) and 'patients' in hospital were redefined as 'customers'. Activities which had formerly had a special identity of their own became disorientatingly subordinated to Business – anyone who travelled on a cross-Channel ferry, for instance, will know how the concept of 'voyage' was converted into a kind of floating retail opportunity. Even isolated individuals became walking advertisement hoardings as more and more ordinary items of clothing were manufactured to carry a written commercial message. Empty churches became converted into supermarkets. The person's lifecycle came more obviously than ever to be marked less by the social and spiritual significance of events than by their market implications. From cot to coffin, the stages of life derived their meaning as much from the typical pattern of purchasing they involved as from any consideration of what Ivan Illich has called 'conviviality'.

Just as the yearly cycle is marked by a series of consumerist celebrations – birthdays, holidays, Christmas, etc. – so the course of our lives has tended increasingly to be demarcated more clearly by the spending sprees they give rise to than by their significance as social rites of passage.

The childhood preoccupation with 'toys' is a good example of this. Given a chance to talk to and occupy themselves with the adults around them, most children are fairly indifferent to toys. However, in a world in which those adults are themselves busily preoccupied with their own corners of the market, children have less chance of socializing than of learning the arts of consumership in their own specially prepared world of toys. Not only do they receive, from the moment their eyes can focus, a training in the acquisition and rapid obsolescence of consumer goods, but they are also inducted into a world of make-believe which offers virtually limitless market opportunities and which may very well serve to detach them for life from any commercially undesirable anchorage in the realities of social existence. For almost all our lives, our market-induced fantasies of how our relations with others, as well as the main events of life, should be tend to obscure the actuality.

There is, in fact, no recess of personal life, however intimate, immune to the intrusion of the market. Sexuality is a case in point. Early in adolescence the addictive power of male sexuality is commercially harnessed to a marketed female insecurity to create a model of 'relationship' which leaves both boys and girls – and later young men and women – at times incapable of controlling and almost always unable to understand both their sexual feelings and their need for intimacy. At worst, youths are reduced to barely articulate chunks of erectile muscle, quartering the Friday night streets in an alcoholically heightened expectation of finding girls they can fuck in a car park somewhere – girls who, again at worst, signal, probably unconsciously, a raw seductiveness no less market-inspired than the romantic love they actually crave. These can appear as people emptied out of their humanity, enacting like sleepwalkers fantasies in which they have been soaked ever since they were small children. They are, of course, not empty of humanity at all. They are like everyone else, human bodies subject to all the pains and longings which are common to human bodies. The difficulty is that they have learned no ways of giving expression to and elaborating their embodied humanity other than those constructed and promoted by the commercial interests of Business.

Very few people have the confidence any longer to allow their subjective experience of their bodies to guide an understanding of their 'relationships'. A woman who doesn't *feel* as sexually rapacious as the heroines of her husband's videos is often easily persuaded that there is something ('frigidity') the matter with her. She is far less likely to take her body as a valid index of the state of her intimate environment than she is to regard it as a substandard commodity. Many women find themselves conforming with a kind of weary despair to the fantasy-infused sexual expectations of their male partners authorized as 'normal' by a commercial world which relentlessly fetishizes sex. And men, as much deprived of an understanding of their own needs for tenderness as of the arts of expressing it, become totally mystified by their female partners' ultimate disgust with and fear of sex. The market defines as 'abnormal' (and hence in need of further consumer activity) states of social and interpersonal being which are an inevitable part of virtually everyone's experience, but which, like not wanting sex, offer no other market opportunity.

It is, of course, not difficult to identify the particular markets which give definition to the various milestones of our lives. In some of the more obvious festivals of the consumerist lifecycle, social rituals seem, in fact, to have given way almost entirely to commercial ones. Marriage, for example, seems more or less to have disintegrated as a meaningful social 'form': its rules, its function, its moral and societal significance are curiously difficult to define or state. By contrast, the consumerist aspect of marriage as 'wedding' has gained a ceremonial precision as elaborate as that of any arcane religious rite. From the wedding dress to the placecards for the reception tables, from the purchasing of the rings to the bridesmaids' bouquets and the booking of the video, the business of getting married has taken on a demanding, deadly earnestness which all but eclipses any other social meaning the act may have. It is almost not too outrageous to suggest that we are close to being able truthfully to say that the point of getting married is to have a wedding.

Infancy and old age are alike in exempting the subjects themselves from being targets of the market – to qualify for that one needs to have some spending power. It is, of course, not difficult to exploit the pride and pleasure of young parents in their new baby (even competing with breast milk may be not so much a defeat as a challenge), but the market opportunities offered by old age have to be established less directly.

Any doubt about the principal function of the elderly in late-twentieth-century British society will be quickly resolved by a glance at their bedside tables or bathroom cabinets. The arrays of bottles of medicine, boxes of pills, inhalers, creams, powders and unguents to be found there give plentiful evidence of the value of old people to our economy. Not to mention all the other institutions of the health care industry (day centres, nursing homes) which will, as chance would seem to have it, in all probability manage to extract their (if not their carers') last penny just before they die.

'Cynical', did I hear someone say? The predicament of the old gives the starkest testimony imaginable to the spiritual profligacy of our way of life. We have no use for their knowledge, for their memory, for their humour or for their love. We leave them as isolated as we dare in cold and lonely rooms where the most they are likely to have for company is a cat, or a weekday visit from the district nurse. And, just as we talk most animatedly about our holidays, or our cars, or our microwaves, they will tell us, if they get the chance, about their operations, their pills, and the progress of their leg ulcers. My point is not a moralistic one intended to stir up shame or inspire new resolves to care. It is rather to indicate the structure of the boat we all find ourselves in, and in which, individually, we shall all eventually founder.

Because the stages of life are given meaning by the consumerist 'forms' which place them in relation to a particular market, and because distal influences are inevitably experienced as proximal or 'internal' events, it follows that a breakdown in the power of the market will be experienced as *personal* breakdown. There is, in fact, one stage of life where the market does seem, at least partially, to lose its grip in this way. The 'mid-life crisis' is not so much a personal breakdown as the temporary absence of a market structure to distract and absorb the energies of post-child-rearing, middle-aged people who have suddenly found themselves confronted by a world which offers little to preoccupy them other than the approach of old age and death. What inevitably feels like a personal hiatus may thus more meaningfully be understood as a gap in the market.

The untapped market opportunities offered by middle-aged people at the height of their economic strength, but no longer with dependent children to expend it on, have not gone unnoticed in the commercial world, but even so it seems peculiarly difficult to identify and exploit a set of needs powerful enough for people in this position to dedicate their lives to satisfying. In this respect middle age contrasts interestingly with adolescence. The insistent self-concern and blossoming sexuality of the adolescent, though often painful enough, are immediately engaged by a market designed to define and exploit them. Through a wide and highly elaborated range of popular cultural media the young person is invited, seduced and bludgeoned into a garish supermarket which positively explodes with sights and sounds offering meanings for his or her feelings and retailing satisfactions of his or her needs. The middle-aged person, on the other hand, steps into no such emporium of excitement. On the contrary, he or she emerges from a marketplace centrally concerned with parenting and family life, and all the consumerist activities associated therewith, into a suddenly silent, almost empty space likely to fill him or her with a mixture of loneliness and confusion.

In the absence of any guidance from the environment about how to conduct their lives – in the absence, that is, of recognizable consumerist 'forms' – middle-aged people have a limited range of options. One is simply to become relatively inactive, self-absorbed and 'depressed', perhaps looking back nostalgically to happier days. Another is to shake free of market influence and become engaged in activities which have social, political or spiritual significances not (yet) easily appropriated by Business (this, of course, is the aspect of mid life addressed with considerable distinction by C. G. Jung). A third is to recycle the activities and preoccupations of earlier phases of the market – the 'second time around' phenomenon which certainly enticed a significant proportion of 1980s middle-aged males.

The seeming inevitability with which so many men during the eighties found themselves circling back to the age of twenty-five almost as soon as they hit the age of forty was on the whole, however, not matched by their spouses. While these middle-aged men, seemingly in droves, departed the family home to set up all over again with women almost young enough to be their daughters, their deserted wives had for the most part no such opportunity. Largely excluded from a sexualized market place which fetishizes only youthful female bodies, no longer centrally necessary to their grown-up or nearly grown-up children, their only possibilities were bitter resignation or, if strengths acquired in their young days were sufficiently developed, a kind of breakthrough into independence and a degree of spiritual self-sufficiency. If one can envisage one class sufficiently extricable from the web of Business Culture to form the core of a counter-revolution, it would probably be that of middle-aged women.

As things are, the market does indeed show signs of trying to organize itself for the middle-aged, and the more it succeeds in doing so, the less, I predict, will be the incidence of 'mid-life crisis'. So far, however, market provision for this age group does not seem particularly imaginative: not much beyond invitations to invest and manage money, buy time-shared holiday accommodation, private health insurance and personal pension plans. Rather surprisingly, the British consumership, during the eighties anyway, still seemed relatively resistant to the option of reconstructing youth through cosmetic surgery, chemistry and prosthesis, though no doubt there was expansion in that direction. Aggressive marketing, one might have thought, might have bitten the ethical bullet and, through PR and promotional campaigns, more actively have developed an advocacy of mid-life divorce and recycled younger adulthood (or at least make-believe versions thereof). On the whole, however, the middle-aged are still a relatively unexploited group, and as such are likely to continue to feel uncomfortably dislocated from market 'forms'.

Perhaps the most important theoretical lesson to be learned from the weakness of the market's hold on life in middle age is the fact of the ultimate dependence of consumerism on biology. If the person is to become locked into his or her essential role as consumer, then consumerist 'forms' have to be linked to biological need. It is, in the last analysis, the body which is seduced into the market's embrace, and it is ultimately the physical sensations of satisfaction which entice us into the glitteringly packaged world of consumer goods.

Consider a little vignette of the mid–1980s. The scene is an inter-city express from Nottingham to London. It is Saturday. A young family distributes itself round one of the tables. A slightly punky young woman with spiky blonde hair, perhaps in her late teens; a young man maybe a year or two older, thick set, with short-cropped hair, a sleeveless T-shirt revealing tattooed biceps and love-bitten neck; a boy of about five, short fair hair and a hard, shrewd gaze; a girl of about nine, apparently too old to be the couple's daughter, with bleached, in places bruised, skin, and an apparently permanent expression strangely compounding supplication and complaint. The table, the rack above them and parts of the seats not occupied by their own bodies are taken up with holdalls and plastic bags. For the entire journey of nearly two hours the older pair converse not at all except to exchange invitations to eat, drink, smoke or hand tabloid newspapers and magazines to each other. The children squabble a little, complain a little, make the occasional demand. Central among the heap of plastic bags on the table is a huge, cumbersome ghetto-blaster which emits the ceaseless chatter and pounding rhythm of popular radio.

There is no point of the journey when all four of these people are not consuming. The plastic bags contain a seemingly endless supply of crisps and canned drinks, cigarettes and packaged sandwiches, plastic toys and puzzle books. Incredibly, at about Bedford, the bags run dry and all four depart for the buffet car to replenish supplies, leaving the radio gabbling and thumping on the table. They are having a happy day out together – they seem relaxed and there is an affectionate quality to their relations which one senses is not always there (the bruises on the young girl's deathly white skin). Though there is very little interaction between them, they seem not disunited: indeed there is something almost determinedly exclusive in the intentness with which they consume, and they are as if encapsulated from the indignant gaze of those other customers of the railway who are forced to consume with them the DJ's babble and computerized 'music' (nobody dares intrude on the idyll – the tattoos and muscular arms bespeak a possible instability it would be unwise to test).

What is this activity which they seem so contentedly to be sharing while, actually, hardly communicating at all? The word springs irresistibly to mind: they are doing precisely what the radio's commercials so insistently recommend – they are 'enjoying'. The journey is one of uninterrupted enjoyment of tastes, sounds, tabloid scandal, the defloration of tantalizingly wrapped packages, the sucking in of tobacco smoke and the excited exploration of new plastic toys. Like piglets at a trough they are united in solitary enjoyment which graphically links physical craving with the 'satisfactions' designed to stimulate it.

Consumption on this kind of scale is, of course, not a matter of spontaneous choice, but is maintained by the institutions of a highly elaborated culture. Indeed, it would not be too far-fetched to identify the family in the train as members of a 'consuming class' which bids fair to replace in societal importance the old 'working class'. Consumption is, of course, not restricted to any one social stratum, but then neither was work. Just as the economy used not to be able to function without an industrial proletariat exploited for the purposes of production, so now, in countries such as Britain, it cannot function without a semi-employed proletariat exploited for purposes of mass consumption. 'Enjoyment' thus becomes the *social function* of the mass of society on which the Business economy depends.

It is certainly in this 'consuming class' that one observes the clearest dedication to, and most assiduous, if informal, training in, 'enjoyment'. There is, for example, likely to be far more emphasis placed on the importance of instant satisfaction in the consuming than in the mediating class. Consuming class people are more likely than their mediating class counterparts to feel an obligation to provide their small children with instant comforters like sweets, to provide the family with a restaurant-type service at meals (with an emphasis on *choice* both of dishes and of the time at which they are eaten), and to make the chief consumerist festivals like the summer holiday and Christmas into occasions for particularly lavish spending. The mediating class – successors to the 'old' middle class – will by contrast lay more stress on the importance of delayed satisfaction to occupancy of a social position which necessitates the exercise of managerial power.

The logic of a consumerist ideology which aims at exploiting the essentially physical capacity for enjoyment of a mass consuming class culminates inexorably in a process aimed at creating addiction. The ultimate market success is to exploit the properties of the human nervous system such that a stimulated 'excitement' is followed by 'instant satisfaction' in a maximally accelerated cycle. Food, drugs, alcohol, tobacco and sex clearly lend themselves admirably to the process of 'addictification', and the challenge to the market resides only in its refining and augmenting their addictive properties (the reduction of food to its most easily assimilable and basically appealing properties – 'fast food' – is an obvious example). Products less directly biologically linked may be sold on the basis of an association with an addictive bodily process: here one thinks immediately of the ubiquitous use by advertising of fetishized sex which has less and less time for romantic subtleties, employing a rapid series of sharp-focused sexual images which punch straight into the nervous system. Alternatively, products not obviously associated with primary biological needs may be rendered virtually addictive through appropriate processes of research and development. Popular music, for example, by being reduced in subtlety and aesthetic demandingness, electronically standardized, perfected, amplified and delivered through systems which cut out or obliterate competing stimuli, manages to hook the consumer into something approaching biological dependence. (To look at the rows of mesmerized customers flicking through the racks of tapes and CDs in the strangely dehumanized mass record emporia found in any city centre is to be reminded of other scenes of addiction – lines of solitary drinkers in 1950s Glasgow bars, for instance.)

Even cultural products designed for the mediating classes were during the eighties marketed increasingly on the basis of their biological appeal. Art, literature, drama and dance, as any recording of an arts review programme broadcast later in the decade is likely to testify, came to be constructed and appreciated on their ability to affect the nervous system of the consumer. The highest praise critics appeared able to bestow on an artistic or cultural production was that it excited, satisfied, moved, stunned or astonished them. Art is thus finally emptied of any pretension to social significance, and is reduced simply to a passive *experience* of an essentially physical state.

The ultimate Business logic is, then, to reduce the average member of the consuming class to an addict of the mass market, locked by the nervous system into an optimally cycled process of consumption, rendered immune to unprofitable distractions, dissociated from any form of solidarity which might offer resistance to the function of enjoyment. The vision is no doubt apocalyptic, but it is one the 1980s brought closer to realization.

Before turning to consider how some of the characters of the decade fared as it progressed, it may be of interest to use the structure of figure 3 in the previous chapter (page 74) to indicate how the theoretical consideration of environmental influence it outlines may assume the features of a given time and place. Figure 4 is thus an attempt to summarize diagrammatically much of what has been discussed so far in this chapter.

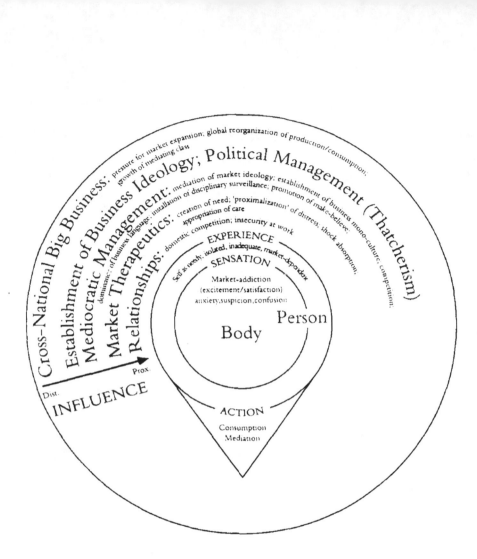

FIGURE 4: The generatioin of distress in the 1980s

II   THE CHARACTERS

Character is, of course, not formed in or by a mere ten years, though certainly the *first* decade of life is likely to be immeasurably more important in this respect than all the rest put together. It is as yet too early to see what the contribution of the eighties might have been to the fundamental character formation of the very young, and I do not wish to imply that the people to be considered shortly, most of whom spent their childhoods in very different times, were irrevocably shaped by the eighties. They were, rather, presented with a problem by the events of the decade which coloured their experience and their conduct with a *characteristic* type of distress.

All six of the characters I shall be introducing felt themselves in some way inadequate to cope with their daily lives, and all blamed themselves for their perceived shortcomings. None considered that his or her difficulties could be attributed even partially to social influences typical of a particular time, and all expected to find what solution there might be to their predicament if not simply 'within' themselves, then certainly within the ambit of their most proximal relations.

A point in social space-time which laid *everybody* low would be unlikely to be seen as causing 'psychological' casualties either because the sources of everyone's distress would be so obvious or because there would be no basis for some people's comparing themselves unfavourably with others. Everyone would be in the same boat, and indeed might derive empowering solidarity from taking arms together against a sea of troubles. Would this not suggest, then, that for only a minority to be disturbed by the times, there must be something 'the matter' with the individuals who constitute it – some weakness not shared by those who cope more successfully?

In my view this would be as strange as concluding that there was something 'the matter' with people who caught smallpox as compared with those who didn't. A society which engenders casualties on any noticeable scale must be found wanting. In this respect the eighties were particularly significant since it was in this decade that all pretence of society's being for people was abandoned: it was now up to people themselves to survive the rigours of the 'real world', and no provision was to be made for 'lame ducks'. In fact, those who, without suspecting it, were injured by the times were far from being lame ducks – often, they were people whose sensitivity, social responsibility and sense of moral integrity rendered them particularly vulnerable to the dishonesty, superficiality and callousness of Business Culture.

It was inevitable that a decade which reintroduced a superficial version of social Darwinism would in a sense render some more 'unfit' than others to survive it unscathed, and if there is any common thread among the stories shortly to be told it is probably that of a lack in the provision in early life of the kind of confidence which, later, helps people to be reasonably certain of themselves in times of trouble. Again, however, I would argue that it is only a perverse view of society which would suggest that this 'goes to show' that the essential question is one of personal weakness: it should be the business of the public sphere to make allowance and where possible to compensate for the inevitable variations in and shortcomings of private experience (themselves, it must be remembered, established under the impress of *social* power), not to exploit and exacerbate them. The characters considered below were all making their way through life as well as it customarily allows until they were confronted *either* by some of the more baneful effects of Business Culture or by a disintegration of 'form' traceable ultimately to that culture.

THE ACCOUNTANT

Dave was slightly bewildered and certainly embarrassed to find himself talking to a clinical psychologist. He was a tall, friendly, good-looking man of thirty-seven. He was wearing a smart dark suit, expensive but not ostentatiously so. While he talked he fidgeted with the keys of his Volvo and looked at his watch at about ten-minute intervals.

His principal complaints were of pains in the stomach and feelings of numbness in the chest. 'My doctor reckons it's stress', he said, but it was fairly obvious from the way he said it that he himself was not so sure. He was more afraid that there was something seriously the matter with him physically, like a stomach ulcer or even a heart problem. He was keen to get to the bottom of things, but he was not used to talking about himself and clearly found it difficult to articulate the subtler features of his complaint. There were, for example, some rather odd aspects to his story which he was obviously as puzzled about as anyone else. He mentioned in passing that he was a keen squash player, and though he had worried about its effect on his physical condition, it had not apparently occurred to him actually to give it a rest for a while – in fact he was playing harder and more often than ever. It was as if, while he was afraid he'd got a heart condition, he actually in some sense knew he hadn't.

In total it took a couple of hours of conversation for a more coherent picture to emerge; coherent, that is, from the psychologist's perspective – though he was willing to give it serious consideration, Dave was not yet quite ready to acknowledge that that was the way things really were. His symptoms were in fact related to the imminence or anticipation of events which he dreaded; they were, that is, manifestations of fear. The events themselves were almost solely related to work, and involved largely two kinds of situations, the first in relation to confrontations with staff who were accountable to him and the second in relation to various kinds of meetings he had to attend, often to give a technical presentation of some aspect of the firm's accounting procedures.

As he began to assimilate and accept the notion that his feelings were to do with fear, Dave was able to reveal an additional problem which had been a considerable source of difficulty and shame. He was desperately apprehensive about driving long distances, especially on motorways. His firm had branches all over the country, and about once every month or six weeks he was likely, sometimes at short notice, to be summoned to a meeting at an office or factory perhaps two hundred miles away. He simply 'couldn't' drive on motorways – his back went rigid, his legs and feet ached so much he couldn't use the pedals properly. He sweated profusely, and started to feel terrifyingly cut off and distant, as if he was about to faint. He resorted to all kinds of subterfuges to avoid having to drive: often he could find a colleague to go with, sometimes he could on some pretext persuade his wife (whom he had not told about the problem) to drive him. If the worst came to the worst he would drive the whole way on secondary roads, which he could just about manage. Whichever way he did go, he arrived at his destination ragged with exhaustion and sick at the prospect of the meetings about to take place.

There were no great difficulties in Dave's home life. His wife had given up nursing to look after their three children, and now that the youngest was old enough she was looking for a part-time job. Their marriage seemed stable and affectionate, though Dave was guiltily aware of having become bad-tempered and less approachable over the previous eighteen months or so; he also had a rather brittle relationship with their oldest daughter, who he felt didn't help enough in the home or work hard enough at school. His wife worried about his symptoms, but knew next to nothing about their causes.

The puzzle, of course, was why Dave's difficulties should have come about when they did. And nobody was more puzzled than he. His success in his career, though not quite phenomenal, had certainly been unusual, and he had risen from a very junior to a pretty senior position within the firm in a very respectably short time, and it was not unreasonable to think of a directorship before too long. He had a secure family life and was socially well integrated. All his life he had enjoyed and was successful at competitive sports, and he and his wife had a wide circle of friends whose company they regularly enjoyed. And then, suddenly and for no apparent reason, he found himself living substantial parts of his life in near-crippling fear.

Someone in Dave's position seeking to understand the causes of his distress is likely to be thrown off the scent by the fact that nothing bad has happened. It is particularly difficult for a man whose life has been an uninterrupted story of success to countenance the possibility that success could itself be a problem. In fact, it transpired that Dave's troubles really started when he was promoted at work into a managerial role which involved the 'presentational skills' of 'image-making' as much as technical ability. Instead of being in charge, as he had been, of a large section of the firm concerned with the production of accounts, he found himself in a position in which he had to represent and explain the procedures involved to others inside and outside the firm as well as ensure that his subordinates carried out those procedures efficiently. He had had to transform himself from a technical expert, a role with which he felt entirely comfortable, into a boss and a front man, both of which roles were completely unfamiliar to him. Instead of making sure things got done by doing much of them himself, he now found that he was called upon partly to bully former equals into getting them done while himself having to represent the results to people (his bosses as well as clients) who were not technically qualified to understand them, but lived rather in a sphere of social influence and manipulation which was quite strange to him.

Dave had been the second oldest of five children, and the apple of his mother's eye. His father had worked as a plumber for a large construction company, and his mother was 'just a housewife', though her father had been manager of a small business. Dave, it seemed, had always been the cleverest of the two brothers and three sisters, and his mother had derived great satisfaction from his success in getting to grammar school. His father had been a quiet, passive man who rarely seemed to be at home during the children's waking hours and who apparently took little interest in his family; he drank fairly heavily and was obsessed with vintage motorcycles, with which he spent most weekends alone in his shed. His wife, though not overtly contemptuous of him, somehow conveyed to her son that she had little sympathy for his father in any particular respect, and Dave himself felt about him rather as of a distant and neutral acquaintance.

Dave did not particularly enjoy grammar school because it was distant from his home and he had few friends there, and felt 'a class below' those he did have. He was successful academically as well as at games, and not unpopular, but neither parent took a direct interest in his life there – his father because, in Dave's view, he had no interest anyway, and his mother because, he suspected, she felt overawed and diffident about getting involved in any way with the school. After passing A levels, the necessity to contribute to the family finances meant that he had to abandon hopes of going to university, and instead he joined his present firm as a junior clerk. He learned accountancy at night school and by correspondence course, and his intelligence and likeability soon set him on a successful path.

All went well so long as he was asked to be nothing other than a highly competent accountant leading a team of other accountants. He had little to do with the board of directors other than meeting requests for financial information. When the company was taken over in the early eighties by an international conglomerate, however, things changed. A new 'dynamism' was introduced in order to achieve a 'leaner, fitter' organization. Dave's old boss, who had been to an extent also his mentor, was made redundant, as were several of his colleagues, and those remaining were required to take on considerably more work. The new top management, as Dave came with only minimal encouragement to acknowledge, consisted for the most part of 'bullshitters' who knew little of the technical sides of the business, including accounting, and Dave found himself increasingly often having to frequent the expensively carpeted offices of board members who needed him to tell them what to say. He was called upon to help entertain clients in a world of fine wines and haute cuisine which he had never formerly encountered, and to attend meetings which demanded a 'high profile' of him since he was often the only one present who had any real grasp of the issues. At the same time, as a new-style 'manager', there came to him with the Volvo an obligation to mediate the demands which organizational leanness and fitness required – Dave had to badger and cajole, bully and threaten people who had previously been friends and colleagues into producing results there was in fact no time to produce.

Dave had never been one to thrive on confrontation. His whole life until the point of his promotion had taught him that success was achieved through conscientious work and amiable social relations. Nor was he one for high living; his was a modest background and he had always felt uncomfortable when out of his social depth, and he had never liked being the focus of attention in large groups. Furthermore, a reticence about emotional relations in his family, especially between his mother and father, had always made it difficult for him to talk about his feelings (there had never formerly been much need) and it did not occur to him that his wife would want to know about or wish to help him with the stress he was experiencing at work.

From his perspective it just seemed that he was failing, and possibly about to fail really spectacularly. He was respectful towards his bosses at work and did his best to learn the new game according to their rules, but the more he tried the more unfamiliar the world seemed and the more gauche and incompetent he felt. His knowledge that often what was being asked of him, and what he was having to ask of others, was impossible led him not to criticize the demand but to reflect even more despairingly on his perceived incompetence.

Because he was not much good at talking about his feelings, Dave was not much good either at talking *to himself* about them, and so he just experienced them as physical sensations, plus a nameless terror that overtook him on motorways.

THE SECOND-TIME WIFE

When her first really bad panic attack struck, Annette thought she was dying. It overcame her while she was waiting in the queue at a supermarket checkout. She left her trolley full of shopping and rushed out into the fresh air; she could scarcely remember how she got home. Her heart was pounding, she was sweating, trembling, unable to get her breath and terrified out of her wits. She suffered three more such attacks – all in exposed public places – before accepting her GP's suggestion that they were indications of anxiety rather than physical illness.

Annette's was not a privileged background. The oldest of four children, she had for as long as she could remember been largely responsible for her brother and sisters while her mother devoted herself to trying to accommodate and appease her husband. The latter – Annette's father – was a gregarious womanizer whose income went on entertaining himself, while his wife trailed round after him in a vain effort to gain his attention and keep his fidelity; when she was at home she complained endlessly and bitterly either to him or about him. Once in a while Annette's father would charm his children by taking them for a weekend outing on which money seemed no object, but for most of the time his attitude was one of irritable neglect, and there was barely enough money to keep them adequately clothed and fed.

Her role as substitute mother to her younger siblings meant that Annette missed a great deal of school. Even so, she passed the eleven-plus exam, but her parents thought it both too expensive and unnecessarily 'stuck up' to send her to grammar school, and in any case the older she got the more she was needed by her mother at home. The first experiences of anxious distress Annette could remember were in relation to the responsibility she felt for the younger children (her parents used to lock them all into the house when the two of them went out for the evening).

As soon as she could (though not having it as a conscious aim) Annette made her escape from the family home. She was conscientious, hard-working, highly intelligent, and pretty – all assets contributing to the possibility of escape. She worked at first in a wholesale warehouse where she soon became a supervisor, and she met at sixteen the man she was to marry at eighteen. She married him because he was kind and attentive, but never really felt strongly attracted to him; indeed strong attraction was not something she experienced until quite a lot later in her life.

Annette had a boy and a girl by her first husband, Alan. His kindness and attentiveness started to wane not long after their marriage, especially as he became more and more absorbed in the small business he was running with increasing success. As time passed he seemed to become remarkably like her father, staying out in the evening and becoming involved with other women; unlike her father he had a tendency to occasional violence. The third time he hit her really hard, shortly after their twelfth wedding anniversary, Annette left him, and went with the children to live with Keith, whom she'd met and fallen in love with some months previously.

Keith was a man who knew a remarkable woman when he came across one, though he could not quite work out what was so remarkable about Annette. He was, in any case, devoted to her even though the speed of her mind often left him standing and the almost painful rawness of her sensitivity sometimes totally mystified him. But what he lacked in mental agility he made up for in commonsense practicality and emotional stability, and they set up house together on what seemed to be a strongly positive note. Money was tight, however, as Keith had left his first wife with their two children and was contributing heavily to their maintenance (his wife had finally moved in with the man she'd been having an affair with for five years).

Annette's first severe panic attack happened eighteen months after she'd gone to live with Keith, and a few weeks before they were due to get married. Even after accepting the hypothesis that she was experiencing anxious panic rather than life-threatening illness, she still had no idea what she could be anxious about. Her unusual intelligence and emotional honesty, however, made clarification relatively easy, and it was not long before she was able to say things which had up until then been no more than vague, unspeakable feelings, laden with dread.

Had they been able to detach themselves from their past, Annette and Keith might have been as happy as couples ever are. Their difficulty was that the small council house they came to live in together with Annette's two children was also inhabited by ghosts – ghosts who, moreover, had a disconcerting habit of materializing in the flesh every so often.

Annette was particularly haunted by Keith's first wife, Janice. The fact that his friends and his parents seemed unable to avoid subtly, and sometimes less subtly, comparing Annette with Janice was little more than a source of nagging irritation; much worse were the effects of Janice's unstable relations with her and Keith's two boys. Every so often she would throw Jimmy, aged sixteen, out of the house, so that he would turn up unexpectedly at his father's and have to be accommodated on the living-room settee until his mother could be persuaded by Keith to take him back.

It took Annette some time to acknowledge that she hated Jimmy. As far as she was concerned he was lazy, dirty, cocky and abusive, but Keith would brook no criticism of him. So Annette spent much of her time rigid with anticipation of his visitations, quiveringly sensitive also to the aura which emanated from Janice (for example, via Keith's muffled telephone conversations with her), for on Janice's whim depended the possibility of an extended dose of Jimmy. Janice herself materialized only very occasionally, at funerals and golden weddings, and Annette did not find her particularly disturbing in the flesh – it was her malign background existence which disquieted her. Jimmy's younger brother Annette found much more tolerable, and so evidently did his mother because he visited far less frequently.

Then there was the ghost of Annette's first husband, Alan, who haunted her through his relationship with their children, especially the younger of the two, Katie, who cried every time she returned from a weekend with her dad and spoke often and appreciatively about him, his ever-increasing affluence, and his unhappiness with his new girlfriend. Annette was tortured with guilt over having robbed her children of their father, and though their son, Robert, had little time for him and was strongly supportive of Annette, Katie's ceaseless remarks turned the knife in her wound remorselessly. Annette had almost no direct contact with Alan, but Katie never lost an opportunity to convey to her her impression of his sadness and that he really missed them all terribly and wanted them back. Alan still sent her affectionate cards at

Christmas and on her birthday – a gesture which would reduce Keith to hours of silence.

Annette's experience as a child had left her resolutely determined never to leave her own children simply to fend for themselves, and to provide for them materially as unstintingly as she possibly could. Not only did she feel that she had deprived them of a father, she had deprived them of a *rich* father, and deposited them in a cramped council house haunted by, and prone to more concrete visitations from, step-relatives they as well as she hated.

Quite apart from all this there was, of course, the question of Keith's relationship to her children. Here Annette was torn between her affection and respect for Keith and her guilt-laden protectiveness of Robert and Katie. An intuitively courageous woman with a sureness of ethical touch in almost every other circumstance, when it came to her own children, especially the sometimes mercilessly implacable Katie, Annette seemed paralysed and without authority. She could not bring herself to take disciplinary action, but nor would she allow Keith to. Despite appreciating and wanting to accede to – even encourage – his wish to 'be a father' to them, she felt they had a right to be protected by her on those occasions when they incurred his quite justifiable and usually mildly expressed wrath. Her ambivalence in this respect caused Keith a good deal of exasperation and frustration, especially when he saw Katie 'walking all over' her.

Annette was not 'neurotic', or 'inadequate', or any of those other things which roll only too readily off the professional tongue. She was a competent, clear-sighted, warmly sensitive woman of unusually strong moral integrity, and while, of course, one could find echoes of her childhood in her present situation of extended and entangled responsibility for people (Keith's children) whose dependence had been imposed upon her, such historical vulnerability cannot in my view be taken as anything like a complete explanation of her panic. She could cope with a lot: with responsibility, with lack of material resources, cramped living conditions, people's hostility, even with visits from the (from her standpoint) loathsome Jimmy. What finally brought her to her knees was not so much 'stress' as an absence of 'form' in which that stress could be cast and given meaning.

There are – for people of Annette's age and social standing at least – rules about marriage. The rights and duties of first-time spouses, parents and children indicate, even if imperfectly, not only how those involved should conduct themselves, but also what it is possible to *feel*. But those rules cannot be extended into a second marriage without incoherent complication. However unsatisfactory first-time marriages may often turn out to be in practice, spouses know, for example, that the 'form' of fidelity makes it 'wrong' to maintain an attachment to another man or woman, and the 'forms' of parental and filial love are also reasonably clearly prescribed. People know when they can legitimately feel jealous, angry, affronted, deprived or rejected. But what do you do about the ghost of a former spouse? Is their ghostly attachment wrong, or simply inevitable? What is the feeling it arouses in you? If you could express it, *should* you? How should step-parents behave towards their spouse's child – as they want to, as the spouse wants them to, as the child wants them to? How should they feel about their stepchild? Should they or shouldn't they disguise their feelings? If so, from spouse as well as stepchild? Annette felt certain about her duties in relation to material provision for her children, even though she could not fulfil them as satisfactorily as she would have liked – the 'forms' in relation to that issue were clear enough. What she (and there are undoubtedly many like her) felt completely at sea over was the *meaning* of her feelings about all the relationships involved, and what she should do about them. Like everyone else in this situation, she had in the end to make up her own 'rules', which after her interlude of panic she managed quite successfully to do.

A society which exalts private individualism in the place of public 'form' often places a crippling epistemological as well as moral burden on those left struggling to find their way: they have to find a language for their feelings as well as guidance for their conduct. And if they fail, they may find themselves simply competing with each other in dumb hostility according to the only rules left – those of the marketplace.

THE AIMLESS YOUNG MAN

It never occurred to Paul to attribute his sense that something was profoundly wrong to anything other than his own inadequacy. Despite having had an expensive education, he was at twenty-one unable to find anything he really wanted to do and had been drifting from job to job – mostly unskilled manual work of one kind or another – at intervals of only a few weeks. His 'relationships' were rather similar. He had no difficulty in attracting young women, but, apart from his relationship with his first serious girlfriend, Amanda, they never seemed to last long, usually because he found quite quickly that he 'couldn't be bothered'. There were times when his lack of direction and general sense of the meaninglessness of things made him quite alarmingly despairing, and he had once (at the time when he was breaking up with Amanda) made a serious attempt at suicide. If a flatmate had not come home unexpectedly, Paul would almost certainly have died from an overdose.

On the face of it Paul was typical of the kind of 'case' which convinces psychiatrists of the validity of their medicalized view of psychological disturbance: he came of a 'good family' and had throughout his life wanted for very little in any conventionally material way, and yet he had never settled down with any energy or enthusiasm to any of the roles which, so far, education and work had offered him. By the age of eighteen he had already found himself in the consulting rooms of a range of medical specialists and psychological advisers who had been appointed by his wealthy parents to advise on the lacklustre performance of their son (Paul had an older sister). His failure to profit from the advantages accorded him led easily enough to the assumption that the trouble must be rooted in some aspect of his biology. The combined efforts of the experts had, however, made very little difference even though Paul had followed their advice and submitted himself to their regimens as conscientiously as he could. He was not a rebel, and would have joined conventional society with satisfaction and relief if only he could have found the right path.

Paul's father was a highly successful businessman who spent a great deal of time flying round the globe and very little in the large house which had been the family home for most of Paul's life. He was a volatile man, not emotionally close to either of his children, and whenever he was at home seemed most preoccupied with extricating himself with as much dignity as he could rescue from the stormy, tearful scenes which regularly took place with his wife. In these, she would reproach him with what she saw as his neglect of his family and with the warmth and generosity which she suspected, but didn't know, he showed to a number of other women in his life. Paul's mother consoled herself during the periods of her husband's absence with gin and tonic and a circle of friends centred round the golf club. She showed an effusive concern for her son's problems, but though he was fond of his mother, Paul found her attentions embarrassing and preferred as far as he could to keep out of her way, which, given the size of the house, wasn't difficult even when he was living at home.

His sister was the person Paul felt closest to and could most easily talk to. She had married a local farmer, and seemed perfectly adjusted to the society which Paul found it so perplexingly difficult to take part in. She would listen for long hours to her brother's rather unsuccessful efforts to articulate his despair, and she racked her brains over courses of action he might take. She introduced him to her own and her husband's friends; she took him to dinner parties and found interesting girls for him to meet; she got acquaintances to offer him jobs in banks, building societies and estate agencies, and she did not allow her frustration at Paul's failure to take advantage of these opportunities, or her husband's eventual irritation with him, to dull her concern.

Paul had gone as a boarder to a second-rank public school near enough to home for him to spend most of his weekends there. The educational emphasis of the school seemed to have been placed on getting pupils into a suitably advantageous position in the business world, and on the whole it had a fairly liberal atmosphere: there seemed to have been little of the pressure-cooked sexuality or sadistic élitism often to be found in such establishments. Paul had, in fact, not actively disliked his time there; he had made some good friends and had been successful enough in the things which mattered to his fellow pupils to be not unpopular. His academic achievement had however throughout fallen far short of what his teachers considered his potential, and it was primarily this difficulty, combined with his apparent inability to 'join in' with real enthusiasm, which occasioned his visits to expert advisers. He failed a couple of science 0 levels, and apart from an A in art only scraped through the rest. His parents bought extra tuition for his A levels, but even so he only managed a low pass in one subject.

In talking about this period of his life Paul was not able to throw any light upon it from introspection. He just never felt he really belonged, like someone standing outside in the cold and looking in through the window of a warm, brightly lit room in which a lot of nice people are having a party.

Capitalizing on his artistic talent, and through the exertion of a little paternal influence, Paul managed to get a place on a course in graphic design in a southern polytechnic, and it was there that he met Amanda. He was bowled over, but also bemused by her. She was, it seemed to him, outrageously unconventional in both her appearance and her attitudes, and Paul could keep up with her only through the pretence of sharing feelings and views which he didn't really understand. Occasional Sunday lunches with her father and her brothers (her parents where divorced) were a nightmare. Her father was a left-wing historian who had a bottomless contempt for anyone who didn't match either his intelligence or his politics, and Paul found himself stretched to the very limit of his ability to dissemble in order not to be exposed as a hopeless bourgeois nincompoop.

There was something about Amanda's world which, even though he could place it in no comprehensible context, Paul found profoundly attractive. Despite often embarrassing if not positively scaring him with her forthright rejection of everything that he had assumed until then right-minded people stood for, it was as if he had at last identified something, though he was at a complete loss to say what it was, which he had previously found missing. Something which had simply been a blank in his life no longer was. But Amanda was a year ahead of him at the polytechnic, and when she left to work in London their relationship survived only a few months. He himself left halfway through his third year, after a spell in hospital following his suicide attempt.

He went back to live at home while he looked for work. He had a number of friends locally, most of whom had well-paid jobs in finance and business, but though he went drinking and night-clubbing with them without real discomfort, Paul still felt on the outside looking in, and, after the suicide attempt, was becoming more and more frightened about his 'peculiarity'. He suspected that his parents' marriage was about to break up, and since most of the time he was alone at home with his mother, he was becoming increasingly uncomfortable about her alcoholically sentimentalized dependence on him. He spent a lot of time with his sister, but felt he was a burden to her.

As Paul, with the latest in the line of his professional advisers, grew more able to articulate his feelings, it became clear that one of the things which most frightened him, and which looking back over his life he had always felt a degree of shame over, was his tendency to what he saw as morbid introspection. He would 'think about' things and people, 'notice' how they interacted, watch and judge the sincerity of the expressions on their faces. He would brood about what they saw in his expressions, and would ponder anxiously – perhaps for almost a whole sleepless night – about whether or not what someone said, or how they had looked, had been 'genuine', and how one could possibly ever know what was genuine and what wasn't.

Paul related these concerns cautiously and shamefacedly, as if he expected to be instantaneously certified insane. When he wasn't, he went on to reflect a little more boldly on the significance of his relations with Amanda. She had, in fact, aroused in him the glimmerings of an idea that it might be possible to lead a life of some real significance and value to others. At a low point of his vocational fortunes he had once even mentioned at home the possibility of looking into social work, but the disbelief and derision he met with had strangled the infant thought at birth.

Paul looked doubtful when it was suggested to him that perhaps there was *nothing* the matter with him, but that he had, with the partial exception of Amanda's, so far simply not been able to find a congenial world to live in, i.e., one which would receive, reflect and even elaborate his interests. He was especially sceptical that incoherent thoughts such as his about 'genuineness' could have been developed by others into a whole philosophy of authenticity, but even so he accepted with some gratitude the suggestion that introspection could be an honourable activity, and that world literature had thrived upon it. To the disbelieving amusement of his best friend, he went on psychological advice to buy a novel by Dostoevsky (an author neither had previously heard of), and he read it with mounting interest. He became more confident in his rejection of the village society which until then he had simply felt excluded from, and began to entertain the idea that there might somewhere be a world he would positively want to join. He began to see that as well as not being suited to be, he did not *want* to be a financial analyst, and probably not a social worker either. He decided to take a year out, drew his savings from the bank, and set off for South America with his still somewhat puzzled friend.

During the 1980s, the suicide rate in England among men aged twenty to twenty-four increased by 71 per cent (*The Health of the Nation. A Consultative Document for Health in England*, HMSO, June 1991). In order not to be aimless, you need a world which has some interest in what you've got to offer it.

THE TRAPPED YOUNG MOTHER

It was not until she was twenty-seven that Dawn plucked up the courage to consult her GP about the panic attacks she'd suffered on and off for almost as long as she could remember. They were a source of deep shame to her. They struck in almost any situation in which she found herself the object of attention – particularly among strangers in public places, but also at work or at social gatherings with people she knew quite well. She would suddenly find herself blushing and stammering, her head would spin, her heart pound, she would feel sick and faint. She felt sure at these times that her distress was glaringly obvious to everyone around, and that they would be concluding that she was either mad, bad or stupid, or probably all three.

The frequency and ferocity of the attacks had increased markedly over a period of two or three months before she went to the doctor, so that she had reached a point where she tried to avoid any kind of public or semipublic appearance which wasn't absolutely necessary. She had stopped going out socially, never went shopping on her own, and did everything she could to avoid contact with people where she worked (she worked three evenings a week as a cleaner at a local school).

Dawn's attitude towards herself was one of utter contempt. The one thing she ought to be able to do, she thought, was look after her children and run the household properly; she'd never had a particularly high opinion of herself, but now she just seemed to be utterly useless. She would have agreed wholeheartedly with the view, had she known it, of a young psychiatrist whom she was referred to that she was an 'inadequate personality'. However, it was only when she encountered a rather more sympathetic audience that she began to articulate some of the background to her distress.

Life was certainly a bit of a struggle, but that was no particular cause for complaint: most people Dawn knew were struggling, some more than she, and they didn't seem to be riddled with anxiety and shame. It was true that Mick, whom she was living with, was out of work, but she could just make ends meet without a wage from him, and he wasn't a bad bloke – he was at any rate kind to her children, who weren't his, and he didn't drink or beat her up, as her ex-husband had used to do.

Dawn had her first baby when she was seventeen and another when she was twenty. She'd divorced at twenty-two and met Mick three years later. She thought a great deal about her children and how to provide them with a degree of stability and emotional security she herself had not experienced. She had come from a large family which had always been materially deprived and riven with violent emotional discord. At one point Dawn had spent three months in care when her mother ran off with a man who turned out to be even less palatable than her father, and her education, if one could call it that, had been ceaselessly interrupted by enforced house moves, parental demands, and occasional truancy. She became pregnant when she was sixteen by the first boy who treated her in what she took to be a loving way, escaping gratefully from the domination of her family. She then lived for eighteen months with her inlaws, with whom she got on well, though her new husband soon proved not to be able to sustain his lovingness – in fact, he was a feelingless, conceited bully whose violence amply exceeded her father's.

Violence, in fact, had not been the main problem for Dawn with her father, who had reserved the full force of his fist for her mother, sisters and brothers. Dawn had, as she put it, been his favourite, but his favouritism had assumed a sexual form which she could well have done without. She hated him with a healthy hatred, but had never been able to reveal to anyone in the family the furtive games he had made her play with ten-pence pieces and the nocturnal 'cuddles' he had imposed upon her. One of her worst worries was how she could keep her ten-year-old daughter away from her grandfather's affectionate embrace, for though Dawn had little time for either of her parents, her family, splintered even as it was into warring factions, was the only source of solidarity available to its members, and they still saw quite a lot of each other. The one person who knew about her father's special attention to her was Mick, but he appeared not to attach very much importance to it, and indeed got on with him quite well – they had several times had a few drinks together.

Dawn was a strikingly attractive woman, but seemed to have little awareness of it. She knew that men often showed interest in her, but even so she had never encountered one who treated her with real tenderness, and she didn't see why she should expect to – on the whole (though it took her some time to see the truth of this) men seemed slightly frightened of her and intent on undermining her confidence in herself. Mick, for example, never seemed to miss an opportunity to remind her of all the things he could do which she couldn't.

Buried deep at the core of her sense of shame was the fact that she was only just literate, and she dreaded any occasion which bore the slightest possibility that she could be unexpectedly called upon to fill in a form or read aloud. Any sign she gave of independence towards Mick would be met by him with a demonstration of his indispensability as a mediator with the official world, and he seemed positively to welcome her phobic anxiety as an indication that she couldn't do without him. She had at one stage plucked up the courage to attend adult literacy classes with a friend, but after two visits Mick found a (short-lived) part-time job, which meant that there was no one to look after the children, and so Dawn had once again to abandon her attempts at getting educated.

She was, however, far from stupid. Despite her profound lack of certainty about her own worth, Dawn adopted a stance towards the world which was characterized by a morally insightful intelligence, and a kind of dogged courage which committed her to a defence of her beliefs even when it cost her agonies of doubt and anxiety. She insisted, for example, on being truthful and direct with her children and protecting them as far as she could from the casual abuses of a world which – she understood but could not say – already had them marked down as exploitable objects rather than privileged subjects. She took a lot of interest in their schooling, and though it was Mick who ostentatiously helped them with their homework, it was she who dragged herself in fear and trembling to school parents' evenings to enlist what support for them she could.

Painfully conscious of her tongue-tied clumsiness in coping with the public side of the family's affairs, and aware (not without a strong tinge of resentment) that she depended on Mick for many such transactions, she failed to realize the degree to which she actually took responsibility for things. In fact, for example, Mick was highly unreliable with money, and Dawn had a constant battle to keep what she earned out of his pocket and available for paying the bills.

It was as if all her life there had been a conspiracy to prevent Dawn from realizing that she was an intelligent and beautiful woman who had a great deal to offer the world. But even though the world for the most part showed a cruel indifference to her gifts, she was constrained to offer them nonetheless in whatever form she could, with her limited resources, devise. The fact that she had never had held up to her the kind of loving and truthful mirror which she so tenaciously kept in place before her own children meant that her courage, though it never died, often failed her.

She was, for example, unable to break her dependence on Mick even though in her heart she suspected that it damaged both of them. She needed him as a front man, but she rejected him sexually with a ruthlessness that hurt him deeply (another example of her stubborn refusal to compromise her core feelings: even though she felt sorry for him, she experienced Mick's advances as a violation of her body which she could not and would not permit). He was terrified of losing her but far too vulnerable to let her see the extent of his need, so he kept her with him by undermining her self-confidence and hobbling her to the household by any means he could find. Because he was, in comparison with the other men in her life, in many ways kind and certainly not violent, she could not understand why she didn't love him – indeed, she was far from clear that she did not.

Her whole life had in many ways been a storm, and her situation with Mick was the safest port she had yet found. She didn't expect any better, and certainly in the social and material seas surrounding her there was to be descried no reassuring lighthouse's beam.

THE MID-LIFE MALE

So far as he could see, life had not been especially unkind to Donald, and he was therefore a little diffident over using the term 'depression' to describe his condition. But that was what his doctor had called it, and he had been prescribed antidepressants, so depression, he supposed, must be what it was. He felt unhappy, certainly, but what seemed to be missing was something for him to be depressed about: he couldn't 'put his finger on it', and it was as much as anything with that aim in mind that he found himself talking to a psychologist.

Donald was not an unreflective man, and not one to run away from his feelings, and though he could see that his life, since his forty-second birthday in 1981, had been in a considerable state of turmoil, he could still not understand why he should feel so desolate and so lethargic, nor why every so often (usually when by himself) he should be overcome by uncontrollable bouts of sobbing over, it seemed, some nameless loss.

Losses there had indeed been, but, though he readily acknowledged their significance, they did not seem to Donald to be the type of loss he was looking for to account for his feelings.

Eighteen months ago he had left his wife and two children to live with Frances, but he did not miss them in the kind of way which would explain his pervading sense of pointless sadness. He saw his children – a boy of sixteen and a girl of fourteen – frequently, and they seemed to be taking the separation of their parents well. His daughter, it was true, had not talked to him for eight or nine months following the break-up of the marriage, and her school work may have suffered a bit, but they were, as he put it, the best of friends now, and what he had feared at the time might be a scene of terrible marital wreckage had proved in the event to be from his perspective surprisingly uncomplicated.

It was only in retrospect that Donald could see how it had all started. He had not been aware of feeling discontented with life, though he had felt frustrated and at a dead end with his job. He was deputy head of a comprehensive school, and unlikely, he felt, ever to be anything else. He lacked the element of ruthlessness he saw as necessary to becoming a head teacher, and in any case was frank about not wanting the responsibility: he preferred being prominent among the led to being a leader, apart from which the job of administrating and managing to the virtual exclusion of all else appealed to him not at all. His wife, who held a position similar to his in a different school, had been completely supportive of his stance in relation to his career, though he felt that privately she had probably been a little disappointed in his lack of ambition.

Donald was a gentle, thoughtful, intelligent man, and though he had always felt a little pained and puzzled by the world's cruelties and uncertainties, he had by no means been rendered ineffective by them. He was sociable, even quite gifted – good at sport, he still played team games at weekends, and he also played the guitar in a small folk group which performed regularly in local clubs. He was passionately interested in ancient Egyptian history and society, or at least had been until the onset of his present troubles, which had put paid to most of the activities which he was not actually obliged to do in order to earn his living.

His marriage to Ruth had been – he would have said at any point – happy and successful. Again, it was only in looking back from his present vantage point that he could see anything lacking in it. They had always got on well, and were even now quite good friends despite the injury he had inflicted on her so unexpectedly. They had both concerned themselves deeply with the upbringing of their children, in which project Donald had assumed a full partnership. Ruth was a practical, down-to-earth woman who accepted the minor peculiarities and foibles of others without censure or complaint, and even though she may at times have wished that Donald could have made a little more time to spend just with her, she never made undue demands upon him. But there had been, he now saw, a certain distance, perhaps a lack of passion between them, which had presumably left him vulnerable to later events.

A similar, though very much more marked distance had existed between his own parents. Thanks to the Second World War, he had seen little of his father until he was five years old, and he and his two brothers had been brought up during that time scrupulously but far from lavishly by their mother, a serious, somewhat anxious woman who, though essentially kind, had been rather undemonstrative emotionally.

Both Donald's parents had been keen for him to make a material success of his life and were acutely aware of the importance of education, not least because they themselves had received only rudimentary schooling. He knew that they were proud and pleased when he got into grammar school (though, characteristically, they didn't show it) and the only real friction that arose in the family was when either he or one of his brothers showed signs of deviating from the path which their parents had tacitly mapped out for them – i.e., of succeeding at school and becoming established in a safe profession. They were, Donald felt, quietly satisfied when he became a schoolteacher, though he did not now feel closely involved with them. He was 'quite fond' of them, saw them regularly if infrequently, but felt that he had little in common with them now. He had, however, been quite surprised at the sympathy shown to him by his father in a recent conversation they had had. He had expected to receive nothing but sharply expressed parental displeasure at his marital misdemeanours, but during the course of an afternoon in the garden his father had managed somehow to convey to him an understanding of his position which made Donald wonder whether his father might not himself have been tempted to take similar steps at some time in his life.

It was Frances who had woken Donald from the slumbers he now saw that he had been in. She had arrived as a junior teacher at his school, and though at first he had considered his attraction to her preposterous, not least because she was thirteen years younger than he, when it dawned on him that his feelings were reciprocated, the two of them became consumed in a blaze of passion he had not imagined any longer possible. For some months he staggered around in a daze, almost mad with love on the one hand and racked with guilt and apprehension for the future of his family on the other. The rather superficial attempts he made to disguise the affair from the rest of the world were far from skilful, and Ruth, with her customarily practical eye, accurately diagnosed his state almost as soon as he had fallen into it. She did not rant and rave at him, but she was profoundly shocked and hurt, though at first Donald didn't allow himself to see just how much. He made several half-hearted attempts to break off his relationship with Frances, but his will seemed to have no say in the matter, and in the end he acceded with little resistance to her begging him to move into her small flat with her.

At first there had been a feeling of almost overwhelming joy at finding himself, as it were, back in his twenties with a beautiful young woman for whom he had become the centre of the universe. Donald was overflowing with tenderness and wisdom, almost ecstatic with gratitude to fate that he should have been given the chance of applying the knowledge and insights of his forty-odd years to nursing this new relationship into an enduring creation of love, free of all the petty blemishes and pitfalls so easily fallen into by the younger and less experienced.

Frances, however, turned out to be less malleable an object of his mature creativity than Donald had led himself to expect. Not only did the inconveniences and material privations of their new life together begin to intrude to sully the idyll, but she proved to be dependent on Donald for love and reassurance in a way Ruth had never been, and though he was still inclined to see this as a positive aspect of their relationship – a sign that it was meaningful and alive – he couldn't deny that it often made for difficulties between them, and occasionally he caught a glimpse of the, so to speak, mechanics underlying their passion.

It seemed just possible, for example, that Frances needed an older, wiser man for a security she had been unable to find with younger ones, and that Donald's age had not been, as it had at first seemed to him, merely an irrelevance to a passion that had grown out of pure ideality. It was with some reluctance that Donald had to acknowledge that there were occasions when he felt that Frances was positively nagging him, and he was rather chastened to discover that the intensity of her sexual ardour had also noticeably cooled. Though he was adamant that his leaving Ruth and the children had been an inevitable, almost necessary event, he also confessed that there had been just a couple of occasions when he had a nostalgic twinge for the peace and familiarity of his former domestic state.

The other aspect to Donald's rather depressed apathy was a restless feeling of unfulfillment. He could scarcely face going into school, and indeed had several weeks off work: the meaninglessness of the routine, the pettiness of the relations between his colleagues, the ever-increasing need for him to be a cross between a businessman and a social worker, neither of which did he feel cut out for, left him longing for a life of greater vividness and significance. Much to Frances's alarm and distress, he applied for a job to work abroad with a Third World population, but in the end didn't attend when called for interview.

Frances wanted a baby, and though at the start of their affair he could have envisaged nothing more wonderful, the prospect of it now made him feel surprisingly tired and old, and his reluctance to enter into the project with any real enthusiasm introduced a little further strain into their relations.

There was a café in the town where Donald lived which was a meeting place for older, mostly retired people who went there in couples or groups to chat for an hour or so. Some Saturday mornings Donald would drop in there to sit at a table on his own and listen to them talking – just for a bit of peace and quiet, as he put it.

THE DESPAIRING OVER-FIFTY PROFESSIONAL

By pretty well any standard, Judith's had been a highly competent and successful career. In her mid-forties she had become the acting head of a small department in the arts faculty of a large university, and had not been made professor only because of the financially straitened circumstances of the institution as a whole and the particularly uncertain status of her department within it: there was a possibility that it might be merged with a similar department in a neighbouring university, or, if things got any worse, possibly disappear altogether.

Judith's fear was that she had become incapable of dealing with the demands placed upon her. She accepted the need to change structures and practices which had since the middle of the century tended to fossilize the academic world, and she did her best to comply with the new managerial demands for the more efficient use of information technology, staff appraisal, the need to attract more students, especially from overseas, and so on. At the same time, she could not but object to any sign of a lowering of academic standards, and she fiercely resisted any innovation which did not preserve the high quality of the department's teaching and research.

Judith was puzzled and upset that she found herself so often in conflict with her senior colleagues over issues about which they themselves seemed in full accord, and she was also hurt and disturbed that her junior colleagues seemed equally often to interpret what she saw as her defence of their interests as a failure on her part to guide the department effectively through the troubled waters of change. She felt weak and helpless, suddenly bereft of the personal resources as well as the professional allies she had previously been able unhesitatingly to call upon.

The striking thing about Judith was how little her current conception of herself seemed to match her actual character. Far from being weak, she seemed a strong and resolute person – positively tough, in fact. She had a fine, quick mind, was clear and positive in her perception and formulation of things, and stuck unerringly to her purpose once she had elucidated what was morally and practically the right thing to do. Not until now, at the age of fifty-one, had she ever really felt profoundly uncertain of herself. She was extremely shaken and frightened to find that on some mornings the very prospect of going into the department made her tremble and weep with frustration and despair.

Not only had Judith developed a successful career as a scholar with a modest but not insubstantial international reputation, she had also been a tower of strength on the domestic front. Her husband was also an academic, but much less successful than she, and had an alcohol problem right from the early days of their marriage. He was a kind man, gentle to the point of ineffectuality, and his drinking had resulted not so much in unpleasantness as in Judith's having had to take almost all the responsibility for the upbringing of their three children. This she had done with the systematic resoluteness – and indeed the love – which she brought to all her enterprises, and they were now successfully established in academically related careers in various parts of the country. They had, as she put it, their own lives to lead, and though she saw one or the other of them quite frequently, she made very little in the way of emotional demands upon them, and they knew little of her current difficulties.

Judith looked after her husband with a tender resignation which had become habitual. She probably knew that his role in the university contributed to precisely the 'dead wood' that the new business-minded management was so eager to excise, but she protected his reputation and minimized the effects of his drinking as much as she could. So far as could be seen, she got no emotional support from him, and indeed he appeared to lean with his full weight on her support.

Judith also had an elderly mother to support. Her father had died in the early seventies, and her mother now lived alone in a bungalow Judith had found for her within easy reach of her own home. Since her mother had become increasingly lame, and also noticeably forgetful, there were few days in the week when Judith did not find it necessary to call in for an hour or so to make sure that all was well.

Though she was a loving, and certainly dutiful daughter, Judith's relations with her parents had not been characterized by great warmth. It had not been so much that warmth had been absent, but rather that, from her parents' side at least, it had been conditional. Her parents, both from the 'respectable working class', had made their only daughter very much the centre of their concern, and had brought her up with the combination of strictness, kindness and impartiality which their unswerving allegiance to Methodism dictated. Judith had always felt utterly certain of them, completely convinced of their interest in her, firmly resolved to earn their approval and acceptant of the justice of its being withheld on those (rare) occasions when she fell short of their standards.

It was not until she found herself in a world that failed to appreciate her industrious intelligence, her moral integrity and her willingness to serve a just Authority that Judith began to see that she did not know how to evaluate her own feelings. For until this time her feelings had always been ratified and approved by others – her parents, the Church, school and university – and those of her private feelings beyond or beneath the interest and concern of this external world had lain largely unexamined, and she was far from sure whether what she herself felt in this neglected domain were things that could and should be felt.

Thus she was not sure whether or not the mistrust she felt for the terms of the new language of management – in which, for example, the avowed pursuit of 'Quality' or 'Excellence' seemed to accompany a diminution in what she had always considered quality and excellence – reflected a justifiable criticism, or whether she had merely somehow missed the point. Such an unaccustomed mistrust of properly constituted authority threw her back on reliance on personal judgements which she didn't really know how to make and couldn't bring herself fully to believe in, and so she simply felt incompetent and 'de-skilled'.

The apparent capriciousness with which new administrative (and sometimes contradictory) regulations were imposed upon her department; the indifference of the new breed of business manager to the failure of the much vaunted 'innovations' to achieve what they were supposed to; the incongruities involved in replacing methods of academic assessment and appointment with 'appraisal' systems of much less depth and substance; the resentment of her departmental colleagues at her earnest attempts to introduce these changes to them as much as at her parallel efforts to protect them from the worst of their effects: all these happenings served to hurt more than anger her, since she could find no point of reference in which to anchor her own view of them. She had become the servant of a master she could no longer recognize, in whose good faith she could no longer trust and who, worst of all, appeared not to appreciate the very attributes of her character which had until then been her greatest strengths.

Although Judith could be witheringly scornful of many of the management procedures she was asked to mediate, and although she on several occasions made herself profoundly unpopular at faculty and other meetings by upholding in the face of what she saw as unintentional Philistinism the academic values she had held dear all her life, she could still not bring herself to believe that the system as a whole had in any degree become destructive or malign. It was above all this inability to diagnose a moral failing in the system which forced Judith to diagnose it in herself.

The incongruity of so competent, strong, resourceful and courageous a woman blaming herself for a state of affairs so clearly perpetrated by others would have been obvious to anyone not blinded by the ideology which had taken such a grip on the decade. The sad thing was that so many of those around her, instead of fanning into life the glimmer of her suspicion that all was not well with the system that had overtaken her, should have treacherously concurred in the view that she was 'getting past it'. Like many women and men of a corresponding age and station in life, Judith found her discomfort and isolation rapidly turning into a longing for early retirement.

CHAPTER FIVE

Help

It is the main argument of this book that emotional and psychological distress is brought about most fundamentally through the operation of social-environmental powers which have their origin at considerable distance from those ultimately subjected to them. It would seem to follow from this that distal causes need distal cures, and it will be the task of the final chapter to suggest what kinds of political, ethical and ideological changes might be needed if some of the worst ravages of our form of social organization are to be avoided.

However, though the reasons for our pained and painful experience may be located far away from us as individuals, we live perforce in a proximal world, and just as the powers which hurt us tend to be mediated by those 'fellow passengers' we actually encounter, so the help we get to relieve or withstand their worst effects is likely to be received from people whose lives in one way or another touch upon our own.

The paradox involved in this state of affairs has already been emphasized: the people who *seem* to be the most important in our lives, those with whom we engage daily in transactions of love and hate, victory and defeat, frustration and elation, are, in fact, but the mediators of powers often so distant in time or space that we, the protagonists, cannot even say what they are. This paradoxical state of affairs applies equally within the realm of psychological help, and much of the difficulty with most approaches to 'treatment' – the unsustainability of claims made as well as the nihilistic implications of some of the blanket critiques advanced – follows from a failure to unravel the paradox.

For it is not that psychotherapy and similar approaches are either marvellously efficacious or dreadfully damaging, but rather that they are at best strictly limited in what they can achieve, and at worst seriously misleading, both theoretically and practically, in their approach to distress. However, it is important to add a qualification to this view, which follows from the premise that counsellors and psychotherapists have very little formal power in relation to those they are seeking to help. As Jeffrey Masson's work in particular has established,[1] psychotherapeutic and psychiatric intervention can be very damaging to the recipient, the more so in proportion to the power available to the practitioner. Psychiatry especially has been accorded sweeping powers over the individual at various times in its history, and though these are probably more in question now than at any previous time, they may still be very considerable.

The critique of psychotherapy which follows, as well as the elaboration of how this form of proximal help may be beneficial, are thus based on the assumption that we are talking about practitioners – whether called therapists, counsellors, psychologists or indeed psychiatrists – who have not been accorded or do not use significant formal power over individuals (for example over their bodies or their liberty). This is not to say that such practitioners have *no* power, and indeed part of my task is to clarify what powers psychotherapists do have, and how they may be used for good as well as for ill.

As I argued at the beginning of Chapter Three, the overestimation of therapeutic power and the failure of theorists of psychotherapy to see beyond the walls of the microenvironment of the consulting room has led to a great deal of misunderstanding about what psychotherapy and counselling can and cannot achieve. If I risk labouring the argument by recapitulating it here, it is because there are, in fact, very few theoretical approaches to counselling and psychotherapy which cannot be fitted into either

1. See Jeffrey M. Masson, *Against Therapy*, HarperCollins, 1989.

or both of two microenvironmental models: that is to say, such approaches try to account for and to 'cure' personal distress which has been engendered in a *world* by both *treating* and *understanding* it within the immediately proximal compass of the patient's intimate relations, particularly, of course, with the therapist.

The first such microenvironment is limited to the space of therapy itself, i.e., the consulting room, and may be represented as in figure 5.

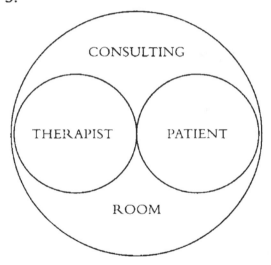

FIGURE 5: The microenvironment of therapeutic space

It is scarcely surprising that where theorists allow their thinking about psychological phenomena to be swamped by their experience of the consulting room they should end up giving the enormous importance they do to the events which transpire between therapist and patient. It is, after all, a world which contains no other occupants. Were the protagonists to be marooned together for a decade or two on a desert island, it might well be the case that their feelings and fantasies about each other, their personal quirks and mannerisms, their expectations, moods and interpretations of each other's conduct would all become matters of large and central significance. However, in a world which permits, indeed demands, that the pair live a vast proportion of their lives outside the microenvironment of their personal encounter, such factors need to be kept in perspective.

The psychoanalyst's emphasis, for example, on the fundamental importance of the 'transference' and on the curative powers of his or her 'interpretations' of it, just like the Rogerian counsellor's concentration on the crucial powers of the 'warmth, empathy and genuineness' of his or her relations with the patient, though, of course, significant in a microenvironment in which little else takes place, are completely dwarfed by the events and relations of the world in which the patient actually lives. Failure frankly to acknowledge this limitation, or even apparently to see that it exists, is, as noted earlier, to court absurdity, and no doubt the touch of ridicule which often attaches to the popular idea of the 'shrink' is brought about by the inflated self-importance of a profession which seems to have forgotten that the world does not end at its front door.

The second microenvironment given consideration by most theorists in the broadly 'clinical' field consists of the personal space in which the patient's difficulties may be said to have developed – the arena of his or her so-called 'psychopathology'. This is often seen as having been most important in its historical aspect, and is once again occupied by a limited number of very proximal influences, as is suggested in figure 6.

It is not, of course, that the mediating influence of parents, siblings and other significant people in patients' past and present lives is not important for an understanding of their psychological development and personal distress. The problem with this microenvironmental model is rather that its obscuring of the influences of a wider world a) tends to give the forces within the microenvironment a dynamism they in fact don't really possess, and b) leads to ideas about 'insight', etc., which extend this dynamism into the patient's present in the form of concepts such as 'will' and 'responsibility'.

In other words, if you limit your understanding of the powers and influences within the world merely to the proximal arena

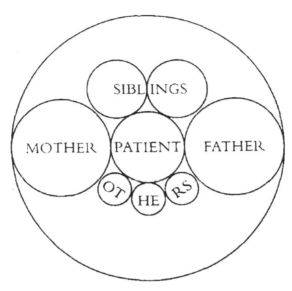

FIGURE 6: The microenvironment of 'psychopathology'

in which your immediate social encounters take place, the *origin* of the activity in that arena will appear to be *inside* the figures who occupy it – for the simple reason that there is no other conceptual space in which it *could* be. It therefore becomes increasingly attractive to believe that activity taking place in the proximal arena is due to the intentions, impulses, desires, unconscious motives, or whatever, located 'within' the principal actors. And once *that* view has been conceded, it becomes convincing to suppose that the individual patient has such impulses and intentions, etc., residing 'inside' him or her and that, perhaps with appropriate guidance from the therapist, he or she can exercise some form of moral choice in changing or adapting them.

Now I am not making what seems to me the dangerous and in fact unsustainable claim that there is 'no such thing as free will'. To do so would invite the kind of fatalism which suggests that 'since nothing I can intend will make any difference, I might as well not bother' or 'I can't help what I do – it's all because I had an unhappy childhood'. Free will, as I suggested earlier in this book and will attempt to elaborate in the final chapter, must exist in the form of a 'necessary illusion' – to act in·good faith human beings must *believe in* a concept of free will. For the psychological theorist, on the other hand, it is not a particularly useful concept, and it is likely to be far more fruitful to consider what patients are able to do about their predicament from the point of view of what powers and resources are available to them to make changes in their lives.

In terms of the help therapists and counsellors may be able to offer patients from the very proximal position they occupy in relation to them, the situation is a very much more modest one than that implied, for example, in the microenvironment of figure 5, and might more accurately be represented by the position as suggested in figure 7.

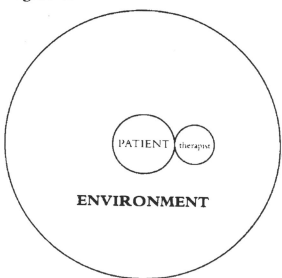

FIGURE 7: Therapy in perspective

The Ingredients of 'Therapy'

There are, it seems to me, essentially three components to the kind of help which can be offered to a person in distress by someone who, though suitably experienced and perhaps qualified in some professional sense, has no powers over that person other than those of persuasion. These are the provision of a) comfort,

b) clarification, and c) encouragement. I shall consider them in turn.

COMFORT

In Chapter Four, I tried to show how easily the therapeutic provision of comfort could be exploited by a Business Culture. This does not mean, however, that such provision is *necessarily* linked to exploitation. It does mean that one needs to take great care to understand the limitations of therapeutic comfort.

There can be few practitioners of counselling or psychotherapy who have not witnessed what often seem to be the almost miraculous therapeutic powers of the 'therapeutic relationship' itself. A patient or client who enters the consulting room for the first time, tense, ashen, eyes dark-ringed and near to tears, leaves after being given an hour of sympathetic listening looking relaxed, pink, eyes bright with rekindled hope.

It is above everything else this phenomenon – the immediate, even physical impact of comfort-giving – which has in my view provided the whole range of counselling and psychotherapy with its principal justification. As always, it is proximal experience which is registered as most powerful by the individual person, and the pain-relieving quality of this form of intimate support is unmistakable to both patient and therapist, leaving both easily convinced of the therapeutic potency of their encounter.

This should, of course, come as no surprise: popular culture is full of expressions which recognize that 'a trouble shared is a trouble halved', that 'two heads are better than one', and that it helps to have 'a shoulder to cry on'. Our whole experience of life impresses upon us the value of proximal solidarity, and the more powerful (or socially highly accredited) the people with whom we are able to establish such solidarity, the more aid and comfort we are likely to be able to extract from association with them. No doubt the mega-rich (or mega-'important') derive great comfort from having in their entourage personal physicians and lawyers (not to mention bodyguards) who are available to share their trials and tribulations at any hour of the day or night.

Our very social existence as human beings, the structure of our bodies and the means through which they are brought into and subsequently sustained in the world *demand* that we have on our side people who will support us. In other words, proximal solidarity is an *essential* form of power without which we would be almost certain not to survive.

There is thus no mystery about the centrality in counselling and psychotherapy of 'the therapeutic relationship', though it has indeed often been mystified and sentimentalized in ways which, though no doubt augmenting professional 'credibility', obscure the very obviousness of the phenomenon of comfort itself. Virtually *any* human transaction is rendered more effective, and certainly experienced as more empowering, if it is conducted kindly and sympathetically.

One must, however, distinguish between the *experience* of empowerment which follows the provision of proximal solidarity, and the processes by which the actual causes of an individual's distress may be removed or modified. Your friend's sympathetic commiseration over your trouble with meeting your mortgage repayments may temporarily make you feel much better, but it won't actually keep the bailiffs from your door.

Just such a confusion between comfort and cure is endemic in the psychotherapies. The person who looked and felt so much better after the first consultation with a therapist will in all probability return a week or two later to say that though the improvement lasted three or four days, it began to wear off after that. For neophyte therapists who have not yet been able to shake off their entanglement in the magical appeal of their profession, this is often a disheartening and worrying experience, and they may find themselves being driven defensively to cover up a sudden doubt about their therapeutic potency. But then they may be reassured as the patient confides a little more, and lo and behold, starts once again to improve under their very eyes. And so it may go on: as long as the patient can maintain contact with the therapist, he or she will feel better, and the longer they are apart, the more painfully will the world re-establish its grip.

What therapists have to realize, of course, is that their contact with their patient is not curing anything, but merely providing a form of empowering proximal solidarity which depends for its effectiveness on its continued existence. There is nothing the matter with this so long as the therapist is able to continue offering support and the patient is able to keep on paying for it. This relationship amounts perhaps to the 'poor person's' equivalent of the personal physician, and for people who have either very few or no other sources of proximal solidarity in their lives it can be of the utmost – even life-saving – importance. The *essential* thing is for counsellors and psychotherapists not to confuse their provision of this service, which may in fact often be the only one they are legitimately able to provide, with some quasi-technical form of effecting 'change' in people.

Received psychotherapeutic wisdom eschews 'dependency' and warns solemnly against creating it in patients; it even assumes a distinctly moralistic tone in disapproving of 'dependency' as an altogether undesirable trait in adult human beings. But this is to miss one of the central points about being human: we are *all* 'dependent' in all sorts of ways, and the question must rather be one of understanding the modes and meanings in our dependencies and with which they occur. It would, of course, be wrong (as therapy could and probably too often does do) deliberately to create forms of dependency in people in order to exploit them financially or in some other way. On the other hand it would be simply foolish not to recognize that our society is a highly intricate network of dependencies which define the very nature of our being.

Inasmuch as the provision of comfort is a, and often the, central component of counselling and psychotherapy, therapists need to disabuse themselves of the conceit that they are achieving anything more grand than giving proximal support to people who for one reason or another cannot get it any other way. The less the availability of such support in people's lives, the more they may depend on its professional provision, and the longer term that provision may need to be. There is no shame, or necessary exploitation, in that. But there is a need for professional comfort-givers to recognize the limitations and dangers of their trade. Several of these come quickly to mind.

First, proximal solidarity is in no way necessarily connected with the distal causes of distress, and is therefore unlikely to be able to modify them. Second, the effectiveness of such solidarity will be in proportion to its extent and duration, and is therefore best provided in the context of the individual's life by people whose availability and commitment are maximally dependable. In this way a counsellor or therapist cannot effectively take the place of family, friends, lovers, etc., and should always be concerned to do everything possible to encourage patients to develop these more enduring sources of solidarity in their lives, thereby rendering therapeutic comfort redundant. Third, though the therapeutic relationship is at its heart a commercial one and should not be sentimentalized, its comfort-giving quality stems from the nature of the participants as people rather than from any technical therapeutic skill. This injects an unusually strong ethical element into the therapeutic relationship, and means that therapists need to consider carefully the implications of withdrawing support from patients for whatever reasons (for example, changing jobs, etc.). Fourth, it needs to be borne in mind that the nontechnical, basically personal nature of the comfort-giving relation means that it becomes peculiarly liable to the kinds of abuses which Jeffrey Masson and others have highlighted.

Priests, doctors and therapists have no doubt all in their different ways contributed to the professional mystification of comfort-giving, but there is really no secret about it. Its essence is to allow another person to *be* without trying to impose upon him or her either a responsibility for being that way or a blueprint for being another way. If you are in pain or distress you are as unlikely to be comforted by the observation that it's your fault as you are by an insistence that you should try this, that or the other solution to your predicament. Ironically, it is often people 'trained' in a helping profession – medicine and nursing are prime examples – who are least good at offering comfort pure and simple, usually because they feel it so incumbent on them to *solve* the person's problems.

But comfort-giving is precisely *not* problem solution, and, paradoxical though it may seem, its very effectiveness depends on its not trying to solve anything. The reason for this will I hope by now be obvious: most of the causes of the kind of distress which puts people in need of comfort are *not soluble* because they are originated by distal social powers which are out of reach of both sufferer and helper.

What we are in most immediate need of as we suffer the torments of a cruel world are *companions* with whom to share our suffering. We need acknowledgement of our condition and affirmation of our experience. We don't need people to press upon us ineffective solutions or blame us for our feelings. The *first* move to be made in confronting outrageous fortune is to stand shoulder to shoulder with others in contemplation of its effects. All too often this is the *only* move which can be made, but even so, so long as it is possible to maintain such solidarity, it is a relief. All you really have to do to establish with someone the beginnings of such solidarity is sit and listen carefully to what they have to tell you, and for that you don't have to be a psychotherapist. But neither, if your are, do you have to be ashamed of it, but merely to bear in mind the modesty of your undertaking.

CLARIFICATION

If comfort is the almost inevitable by-product of virtually any form of sympathetic helping, some version or other of clarification constitutes the core of nearly all psychotherapeutic 'techniques'. The wizardry of the therapist consists in his or her being able to penetrate patients' confusion in order to reveal to them the 'real' reasons for their distress.

It is in this process of clarification that practically all of the mystique of psychotherapy is contained. The arrogance of the therapist who claims to be able to 'tell at a glance' the nature of patients' relations to their parents (as for example Masson reports of Jung, *Against Therapy*, p. 158) is matched in propensity for myth-creation by the popular conception that psychologists can 'read the minds' of anyone their eyes happen to fall upon. We move, so it would seem, in a web of self-created illusion which veils a secret, *interior* space where our (thanks to Freud, largely dishonourable) motives wait to be discovered by a knowing clinical gaze.

Slightly more soberly, the process of clarification is most usually seen as one in which people's moral equivocation over the 'real' reasons for their conduct is resolved through the patient and skilful work of the therapist in revealing their origin. In this way, in psychoanalysis, for example, a patient's current concerns, perceptions and actions may be 'interpreted' in terms of the emotionally (sexually or aggressively) laden situation in which they originated; the sex or aggression is, of course, most likely to be construed as in some sense 'belonging' to the patient. Having thus had revealed to him or her the somewhat murky motives which lie behind the fog created by 'repression', the idea is, of course, that the patient sees, literally (though analysts are not bold enough to put it so bluntly) the error of his or her ways, and becomes at last able to live in the pure reality of therapeutic revelation.

Therapists have, of course, noticed that insight into the origins of 'neurotic conflict', etc., does not always lead automatically to an abandonment of the strategies it has engendered, but they have not on that account put any less effort into the therapeutic work of clarification. In one form or another the notion that people should, once they've seen what they've been up to, be able to adjust their conduct to more favourable or acceptable goals seems to be one that therapists simply cannot relinquish.

The observation that 'intellectual insight' – the more theoretical appreciation that such and such were the reasons for one's present state – did not seem to produce a change in that state led to the concept of 'emotional insight' in which one was supposed really to feel *impelled* to change through the force of the emotional impact of a revelatory experience of insight. But, as I have pointed out earlier, there is no particular reason why a change of heart should from any theoretical or practical point of view be any more or less effective than a change of mind.

The importance accorded by the psychotherapies to an understanding of the origins of one's condition does not necessarily stem from the kind of psychoanalytic creed that one may, through the process of insight, become free of morally dubious enterprises on which one has been engaged since childhood. An alternative, seen for example in various versions of 'cognitive therapy', is that current conduct is a product of beliefs or attitudes which, far from being necessarily grounded in some prototypical childhood experience, may be acquired almost accidentally, and certainly potentially interchangeably. In this case clarification of what patients believe – what are their 'cognitions' about their conduct in relation to their world – is important principally so that one belief can be substituted for another, more adaptive one. In this kind of approach the *origins* of patients' cognitions are far less important than the nature of the cognitions themselves, and it is *this* which needs clarification. In this way, for example, it may be seen as much more important to point out to someone that he or she resists venturing into new social situations out of an expectation of ridicule (and to replace it with an expectation of approval) than it would be to lay bare the origin of the sense of ridicule.

Whatever the debates and differences among the various brands of psychotherapy, however, they all in one form or another find it necessary to enter with the patient into a process of clarifying the 'true' nature of his or her enterprise. This procedure is likely (as in the case of 'insight' therapies) to be seen as in itself therapeutic, or (as in the case of 'cognitive' therapies) essential as a preliminary to installing the attitudinal equipment necessary for alternative enterprises. In any case, the emphasis is understandably enough on the potential of the clarificatory process to result in therapeutic improvement; to form, that is, the main technical procedure through which, within the context of the consulting room, the therapist can work the magic of change.

The point I wish to make about this is not that clarification is in itself necessarily misguided or morally undesirable, but that there are within this general area both epistemological and ethical confusions which may be avoided only if the process of clarification is placed within a coherent theoretical context which takes proper account of its strictly limited *therapeutic* significance.

Of course in the understanding of distress it is important to explain how it came about, but, equally obviously, such an explanation, however accurate, does not lead automatically – or in many cases even conceivably – to a change in the conditions which created the distress in the first place and maintained it thereafter. Even if there were such things as changes of heart following from insights into the moral wellsprings of one's conduct, it is far from clear how that might enable one to conduct oneself differently. It is even less clear what the relation of people's conduct is to their 'beliefs' or 'attitudes', or why, if such things are fundamental, they should be any easier to change than the conduct itself.

All the motivational bits and pieces of machinery which are supposed to clutter our interiors and which therapeutic clarification is supposed to reveal – the unconscious wishes and complexes, the impulses, the attitudes and beliefs – are on the whole left unanalysed by the approaches which postulate them. This is in my view bound to be so because they are cut off from any environmental context which would make their explication possible. They are, in fact, inward projections of distal outer influences which are overlooked by therapists mainly because they so obviously display the limitedness of the therapeutic enterprise. If the causes of your distress are not inside you, but relatively far off in environmental space-time, can you really be expected to do anything much about them?

There is indeed a point to helping people clarify the grounds of their distress; it is not, however, to place upon them the burden of responsibility for it, to imply that it is a matter of their mistaken perceptions, their infantile immorality or their inappropriate attitudes, but to help them achieve an accurate view of how they have come to be affected by the field of power into which they were thrown at birth. From this perspective *the point of therapeutic clarification is to undo the mystifications of power.*

Of itself the process of clarification makes absolutely no difference to the person's distress, since of itself an appreciation of the nature of the influences on one's life carries no *necessary* implication of being able to do anything about them. But there is at least likely to be some ideological advantage to knowing where one stands in relation to the operation of past and present powers, and it may, of course, be that in practice one can do something about some of them.

People may be mystified about the reasons for their distress in three main ways: either they a) cannot *remember*, or b) cannot *see*, or c) cannot *say* how something came about. The concept of 'repression', with its unnecessary moralistic overtones (that the person manages to hide from him/herself a morally unacceptable thought or impulse), would seem to me better replaced by one which, as I am suggesting, emphasizes the contrary notion that something has been concealed from or forbidden to the person.

a) Being unable to remember

Whether or not someone can *remember* the origin of their distress will depend upon whether it falls within their available span of memory. This is the temporal equivalent of the spatial power horizon. The impress of power is perhaps particularly strong when it takes place before the person is able verbally to reflect upon and rehearse the events of his/her life (i.e., during infancy). As with so many of the concepts in which it deals, psychoanalysis manages often to moralize the faculty of memory by implying that if you cannot remember childhood events it's because somehow you have chosen not to. As I have already suggested, however, a memory which has not been verbally encoded remains embodied as a *feeling* which simply cannot be turned into a coherent account.

In Chapter Two, Susan provided an example of how this kind of incoherent feeling may dominate a 'clinical condition' such as an 'eating disorder'. Susan did not contain within her a greedy, wilful infant who somehow needed to be brought to book, but had impressed upon her *as* an infant embodied practices which she just could not say anything about and upon which she could gain no critical purchase. She literally could not remember the origins of her feelings, and no amount of 'interpretation' could have made her remember them. They could only be reconstructed as a hypothesis which more or less fitted facts which *could* be remembered or otherwise ascertained from data available in the present.

Clarification of events beyond the span of memory is thus a matter of inventing a 'likely story' which accords as closely as possible with what can be known. Its value lies precisely in *weakening* the sense of guilt which is often instilled into small children along with the exercise over them of adult power and which accompanies the feelings that remain at the base of their experience ever after. It may at least be preferable to be in possession of an only partially supported hypothesis that there was a 'good' reason for one's pain than for ever to bear the burden of an original sin one cannot remember committing.

b) Being unable to see
I have already discussed at some length the way in which people may not be able to *see* the reasons for their distress because of

the limitation placed on their view by the 'power horizon'. One often cannot know – and in the past could not have known – the causes of events which originate in distal environmental space and reverberate through the field of power until they are mediated proximally right up against our bodies, simply because those events take place too far off for our understanding to reach. In principle, the explanation for many of the things which end up giving us pain may be quite simple, but will in practice be almost impossibly obscured by the complexity of the transmission of social influence through environmental space.

The point I wish to emphasize is that, though complicated, impossible to see as well as hard to trace, the reasons for much of our activity and experience are not in the least mysterious in the sense that they originate in some murky inner gloom which only the beady eye of the expert can pierce. Much of the time, to be sure, we don't know what we're doing or why, but this is not, as it is so often taken to be, a *psychological* mystery of the 'unconscious mind', but the rather prosaic result of our being unable to identify the environmental influences which operate upon us.

The trouble is that we confuse the *mechanics* through which we react transitively to environmental influence with the *causes* of our actions. We experience events largely through our bodily sensations and we assess their nature and significance through the psychological apparatus – the meaning systems – which individually and collectively we have developed. We then mistakenly assume that what we feel, believe and know about the processes of our reacting to the world is all there is to know about them, *including* their causes.

Geoff, in Chapter Three, thought that he was in possession of a more or less complete explanation of his distress in relation to being dismissed from his job, much of which referred to the feelings and intentions of himself and those around him, but, of course, no causal account of those events could be complete without an analysis of business policies and activities of which he could have had no conception. In many ways the means through which environmental influences are mediated – for example, the events in the nervous systems of individuals caught up in them and their conscious appraisal of them – are mere details (if extremely complex ones) in a causal process of much more fundamental importance. Therapeutic psychology, if it's not careful, gets so bogged down in these mere details that all it does is compound the confusion of those it seeks to help.

People who consult psychological experts frequently want and expect their distress to be ended by being shown how they can work on the processes 'inside' them which, in their and too often also the expert's view, bring it about. If they have a biological bias they will want a pill, if psychological a formula or procedure which will somehow switch off the pain. This is about as sensible as trying to 'cure' feeling cold by suppressing your shivers.

Much of the time I spend in 'clinical' consultation with people is in trying to persuade them that there is nothing wrong with them, and that rather than trying, metaphorically speaking, to suppress the shivering, or blaming themselves for it, they should look around to try to identify the reasons for it. Because it runs so counter to so much of our 'psychologizing' culture, and because also it highlights the limitations of therapeutic power, this is often a surprisingly difficult task. When successful, however, it may help people to feel a little better about themselves if only because, again, it lifts a moral burden from their shoulders: at least they don't have to feel that their condition is 'their fault'.

It is, of course, not often that a clarification of someone's distress which enables him or her better to see into the nature of the influences causing it leads to any greater possibility of his or her being able directly to do anything to affect those influences. It may occasionally be possible for people to identify influences which are proximal enough for them to act upon them directly, for example, by negotiating a new relationship with an immediate superior at work. It may also be possible for someone to develop strategies which subvert the influence of powers which cannot be modified in any more direct way.

For example, many of those in the 'despairing over-fifty professional' bracket could use a 'demystified' understanding of their predicament simply to ignore demands made upon them. Where such demands were the product of make-believe, or of rapidly changing and extremely short-lived managerial fashions, bundles of papers could safely be consigned to waste-bins without the threats they contained or the enervating procedures they required ever materializing.

On the whole, however, few people can through the process of clarification become aware of much more than the fact that the events out in environmental space which constitute the ultimate causes of their distress, even if they can be seen, cannot be touched. This is a matter for despair only for those professional helpers who depend for the justification of their activities on an essentially magical conception of 'psychology' – for example, that the world can be changed by the power of thought. Most 'patients', in my experience, are relieved to have their personal competence, i.e., their moral viability as human beings, restored to them even if they are no more able than before to get at the causes of their troubles.

c) Being unable to say

The third principal source of confusion over the reasons for distress centres round what people cannot *say*. This probably conforms more closely than the other two sources – what lies beyond the span of memory or over the power horizon – to the conventional concept of 'repression'. The latter, however, as I have indicated, tends to suggest that if something cannot be said it is in some sense or other because the person does not *wish* to say it (even if the 'wish' be an unconscious one). My point, rather, is as always to shift the dynamics of this kind of process from the individual to the field of power in which he or she exists.

One of the main ways in which 'big' people exercise tyranny

over 'little' people (and, of course, maintain thereby their relative advantage) is by placing an embargo of some kind on 'little' people's ability to criticize the mechanics of their oppression. A child very quickly learns what it can and cannot say, and if adult censorship is impressed upon it with sufficient ferocity, it may well come to be unable to speak a forbidden text even to itself. (It was, once again, typical of Freud's disciplinary moralizing that the concept of the 'censor' in repression was placed *inside* the person, so that instead of being a victim of oppressive power, he or she becomes the neurotic editor of guilty impulses.)

There is nothing strange about becoming unable to say to oneself what one cannot say (because it is forbidden) to others. 'Thinking', in the sense we most usually give to it, is nothing other than talking to ourselves, and we talk to ourselves in exactly the same ways and for exactly the same reasons we talk to others (the Russian psychologist Vygotsky[2] gave helpful accounts of how these processes develop). We are not split psychologically into two realms in which entirely different rules apply: an outer realm where we use a special language of diplomacy, and an inner realm where we confide to ourselves the real truth. The rules which govern our talking to ourselves, though, of course, we may apply them differently, are exactly the same as the rules which govern our talking to others (and they to us).

It follows, then, that if the impress of power is used sufficiently heavily to reinforce an interdiction upon a particular utterance, we will be as unlikely to utter it to ourselves as to anyone else, especially if, as in the case of the small child, we have not yet been able to perfect the skills of concealment and lying. It is a familiar part of everyone's experience that the social context in which one finds oneself is a powerful determinant of what one feels able to say. It takes an unusually brave person to point out that the emperor has no clothes to an audience who do not wish to hear it, and the fact that after a time even that person becomes

2. See his *Thought and Language*, MIT Press, 1962.

unable to *think* the word 'naked' is an indication, not of creeping cowardice, but that language (and hence thought) are not our personal, interior possessions, but part of a culture we share with others. If, for example, the Business language of the eighties continues to be parroted for long enough by enough of us, and to be backed by the institutions of power, before much longer we shall be able to speak nothing else.

Whoever controls language, then, to a great extent also controls thought. In this way, as Foucault has established, the very nature of knowledge is bound up with the authorization of power. People who are submerged within a particular field of power often have great difficulty in giving credence to ways of speaking and thinking which originate from anywhere outside it. For example, a company man who had as part of his 'appraisal' been given a psychometric test which labelled him a 'thinking introvert' (and therefore rendered him, it was supposed, of doubtful potential as a salesman) became immediately profoundly pessimistic about his prospects, despite having spent the previous fifteen years successfully selling. The context of power in which his 'personality' had been 'measured' and the label fixed authorized a view of him which no amount of experience seemed able to gainsay.

In the same way, a particular context of knowledge acquisition – a university education, say – doesn't so much liberate the mind for a disinterested contemplation of truth as authorize through the impress of power a certain type of analysis and criticism. 'Knowledge' – what we can legitimately expect to be able to say which will command a respectful hearing – cannot be separated from the mechanics of power.

One of the problems faced by a psychologist or psychotherapist concerned to 'demystify' such processes illustrates this very point: he or she is likely to be speaking from a standpoint not authorized in patients' experience. Patients may simply feel that, although they can see the logic of therapeutic advice which runs counter to the received ideology of medical authority, it lacks sufficient 'credibility' for them to be able to act upon it.

However, the fact that something cannot be said, or that only certain kinds of things *can* be said, doesn't necessarily mean that it doesn't exist. Whatever the community might say, the emperor *is* naked, and it may only take a shift in the structure of power which ties everyone's tongue to enable his state to be openly remarked.

It is perhaps not surprising that the therapeutic concept of 'repression' has concentrated so heavily on what cannot be said, since the 'lifting' of such repression is the only form of clarification likely to be of direct and immediate benefit to people. In other words, helping someone to speak a truth which is or had been otherwise forbidden to them may be a source of enlightenment which really is empowering.

Steve, for example, was totally at a loss to explain his irritability at home. This had occasionally developed into outbursts of violent temper during which he had hit his wife or subjected his son to a vicious verbal assault. He was deeply ashamed of these incidents and extremely worried that his marriage would disintegrate as a result. He put it all down to stresses at work and wanted to know if there were any techniques of relaxation or self-control which could prevent further lapses.

As often seems to be the case with people who simply cannot say what is happening to them, an examination of Steve's circumstances was extremely puzzling – there seemed to be absolutely no reason for his state. He had, it was true, had some quite serious problems at work, but these had been resolved months ago. He was devoted to his wife and family, and there was no obvious sign of his own family background having been in any way disturbed. It began to seem as though there must be some demon inhabiting him, some interior fault or 'dysfunction' to account for the terrible disturbances in his otherwise almost unusually untroubled life.

However, reading between the lines of the account he gave of his early life yielded one or two clues to the nature of his difficulties. His description of his parental upbringing as loving and supportive and his boyhood relationship with his sister as 'brilliant' at first diverted attention from a state of affairs which was in truth very different. It was only when he let drop that his father had died of a liver complaint, and that he had not seen his sister for a 'few years' despite her living in the same town, that more persistent enquiry revealed that his father's liver complaint had been cirrhosis and that he had been an alcoholic with a 'very nasty' temper, and that Steve's sister had been the overwhelming favourite of his mother, with whom she had shared a life-long contempt for almost everything Steve thought and did.

Neither his father's drinking nor the bitter rows it provoked with his mother had ever been directly alluded to in the family, and it was only in talking about them to his psychologist that Steve began to acknowledge that they 'must have been a problem'. But before he could voice such criticisms, he had to be, so to speak, offered a language in which to do so. It wasn't, of course, that he literally didn't know the words, but rather that he had not been accorded the authority to apply them to his experience in the way that the psychologist was suggesting. Even with practice, he clearly found the exercise a strange and unfamiliar one.

Having come to grips with the historical embargo on telling the truth to himself about his early family life, Steve found it much easier to assess his current position more accurately, and he was quite quickly able to confront features of his marital situation which until then he had simply avoided talking to himself about (the fact, for example, that for the last six years his wife had completely withdrawn from him sexually). Being a capable and resourceful man, Steve made good use of his new-found power to tell himself the truth, and had no further need of psychology. He was no longer surprised by his bad temper, and discussed quite amicably with his wife what course their futures might best take.

Although sometimes difficult to identify (simply *because* the person cannot say it) interdictions on utterances of the kind which caused Steve his problems are relatively easy to lift. By their very nature they usually involve only the most proximal sphere of the person's relations – often, of course, in the past – and so are held in place by no very great or inaccessible social influence. The power of the therapeutic alliance in such cases may well be enough for the person to use an accurate analysis of his or her situation to act directly upon it.

I cannot say, however, that in my experience this kind of personal dilemma (in contrast to the *societal* control of meaning and authorization of knowledge) is so often to be found at the root of people's problems as the therapeutic literature suggests. Most of us who survive childhood have managed to find ways of saying what our parents forbade us to, and will quite early on have been able to abandon the necessity for the kind of despairing, 'don't-know' muteness one sees in frightened children, perhaps to develop instead strategies whereby we are able to lie to our parents while telling ourselves the truth. (Lying, I have often found, is a skill necessary to the avoidance of oppression, and if people can't do it, they need to be taught.) Far more usual as causes of lasting distress are those which are beyond our reach in space or time.

ENCOURAGEMENT

Most psychotherapies lay very little theoretical emphasis on the necessity for people to grapple with those material structures in the outside world which have contributed to making their lives a misery. Therapeutic change, it appears, is wrought within the walls of the consulting room. Of orthodox individual therapies, only the behavioural approach takes proper account of the influence of an environment beyond those walls, but even in this case such influence is seen as almost entirely intransitive: patients are not so much expected actively to get a grip on the world as to be submitted to processes of 'conditioning', 'contingencies of reinforcement', etc., which will be devised by the therapist. As with the 'psychodynamic' approaches, this again has the merit of preserving the status of the therapist as expert and the process of treatment as technical.

It seems likely, however, that despite their theoretical indifference to the outside environment as a factor in therapeutic change, pretty well all experienced therapists will in practice, though very probably unknowingly, accord it quite a lot of importance. Having established a relationship which provides patients with a degree of comfort, and having clarified as far as possible the nature and causes of their difficulties, the obvious problem remains of considering what they should do about it all.

Again with the exception of the behaviourists, the interesting thing about psychotherapists and counsellors is that they don't even pretend to know what people should do to make changes in their lives. The difficulty, no doubt, is that once again the barely formulated idea at the back of therapeutic thinking is that 'change' is a matter not of changing a *world*, but of bringing about some kind of 'intrapsychic' event which will fill people with new resolve, transform their attitudes, expectations and beliefs, or adjust their perceptions of the past – in short, operate in some way on those internal moral and psychological forces which are supposed to 'cause' our 'behaviour'. Even where behavioural therapists acknowledge that the person is related to and shaped by a world, their therapeutic imagination doesn't seem to stretch beyond a vision of shaping the patient in a new way by setting up the necessary reinforcements.

So when it comes to doing something about the predicaments that people find themselves in, the conventional therapeutic answer seems to be that they should either be exhorted, persuaded or conditioned into taking a new tack. The world will not budge, so the patient must 'adjust'.

If, however, we are not independent moral entities, and if therapeutic microenvironments cannot legitimately be detached from the influences of the wider environment in which they are set, then therapeutically inspired resolve and consulting-room experiments in conditioning are not going to be enough to make any real difference to people's troubles. We need to realize that, rather than the patient being a problem for the world, the world is a problem for the patient. We are the embodied products of environmental space-time. To make a difference to our lives we need to be able to exert what little influence we have on the environment to make it, from our perspective, a little more benign. It is not *we* who need to change, but the world around us. Or to put it another way, the extent to which we are able to change will always depend upon some material change in the environmental structures of power which envelop us (and insofar as these cannot be changed, for example because they are in the past, neither can we be wiped clean of their effects).

The difficulty with this is immediately apparent: how do we, relatively powerless creatures, bring effective influence to bear on the environment? It is this difficulty which accounts for the therapeutic silence on *how* to confront the causes of our distress. Since they have no particular knowledge of the procedures of getting to grips with and modifying the baneful influences of power, counsellors and psychotherapists are reduced to *encouraging* their patients to do the best they can. There will, of course, be times when an experienced therapist may be able to suggest courses of action which have served patients well in the past, but this kind of knowledge remains completely informal and unelaborated, and will continue to do so as long as the therapeutic profession shirks the theoretical task of emptying people of all the intrapsychic contents it has stuffed into them and putting them back into a coherent relationship with the environment. Even the achievement of this aim, one should note, would be less likely to extend the sphere of therapeutic influence than to define more accurately its limitations.

If you wanted to learn to play the violin, you would be well advised to seek out a teacher who knows how to play one, who is acquainted with the *materiality* of the instrument, its sound, its feel, its relations with the body. The teacher should know not only all this, but also how to impart such knowledge to the pupil –

how, for example, to reproduce in another person the body-instrument relations known so well by him/herself. The teacher thus puts the pupil into a new set of relations to a world the pupil has not previously encountered. What such a teacher does *not* do is talk endlessly about how to play the violin, or merely exhort the pupil to play, or assure the pupil that he or she *can* play, or train the pupil to *imagine* being able to play, or offer a course in hypnotic suggestion that the pupil is already a virtuoso.

The project of the psychotherapist (and perhaps as much as anything it is this which reduces it in any ultimate sense to absurdity) is, of course, considerably more ambitious than that of a music teacher. It's hard enough to acquire, refine and communicate the kind of knowledge you need to teach someone to play the violin. What do you have to know to become an expert in living life without distress?

Psychotherapy's 'credibility problem' is by now familiar. The ideological enterprise of psychology and psychotherapy has been to detach person from world so that social exploitation can be represented as personal breakdown. Therapists who unwittingly mediate this process, even when they can see that their patients have been injured by a malign world, and even if they cast around for effective procedures which they can encourage patients to adopt, are likely, because of the impossible grandiosity of the aim, to find themselves falling back helplessly on the magical tradition out of which their profession grew: the belief in personal transformation following upon a form of ritual consultation with a charismatic expert.

However, it has not always been and is not everywhere quite as muddled as this. The importance of the environment in the constitution of human character has been a theme of philosophical and psychological thought throughout history, and it may well be only in the twentieth century that it has become quite so distorted and submerged. In the *Republic*, for example, Plato's concern with the kind of environment which would produce his ruling class is meticulous, and a preoccupation with the arts necessary for shaping a desirable life was, of course, common in Greek thought. In the present day, 'psychology' of this kind has, ironically, passed out of the official discipline of psychology and become the informal practice of politicians and business people who set about engineering the kind of society it is in their interest to produce. It is only in the new, and so far 'low profile', development of 'community psychology' (and even there not everywhere) that serious thought is being given to the relation of the individual experience of distress to the social structures of power which cause and maintain it.

I do not wish to imply that there is no value at all in the therapeutic encouragement of patients to try to grapple with the proximal mediation of their difficulties – I have already acknowledged that there may well be empowering aspects of patient-therapist solidarity. Encouraging patients to challenge people who have so far exacted unquestioning submission, to risk situations which have always been avoided, to learn procedures which have previously been feared, and so on, is likely to be recognized by nearly all therapists as something they spend a lot of time doing. Often such forms of encouragement are likely to be dressed up in a technical guise, as, for example, 'assertiveness training', 'systematic desensitization', 'anxiety management', etc.

But the fruits of such enterprise are as limited as they are because the field of power in which we are caught is relatively so impervious to our attempts to act transitively upon it. There are useful adjustments which people can make – for example the woman who fearfully challenges her husband's domination to find to her surprise that, even if reluctantly, he gives way; the man who finds that abandonment of a macho posture brings relief rather than defeat – but on the whole the distal influences which transfix us through their proximal mediators are not moved by such tactics.

An important part of assessing the changes people can make to their lives is to establish what powers and resources they have available to bring to bear on their environment. It is remarkable how little detailed research has been carried out in this area, and yet in my experience it is *always* the case that useful 'therapeutic' gains are made only by people who have the resources to make them. The more one is able to reach out beyond the immediate proximal influences on one's life to impinge upon the structures which control them, the more chance one will stand of being able to relieve the distress they give rise to. The means which make such reaching out possible are, of course, precisely those which people have down the ages tried to appropriate in order to establish or maintain social and material advantage: money, education, association with powerful individuals or groups. There are also, of course, the personal – even biological – characteristics which may be exploited or bartered in pursuit of such material forms of power – for example, intelligence, physical strength or attractiveness. A therapeutic approach which maintained that you could effectively influence your world without *any* of these (for example, by tapping some form of 'inner strength') would be not only stupidly sentimental, but ideologically very damaging.

Before encouraging someone to set out in an attempt to make changes to their world, one needs, then, to establish what resources they have to back them. If they have none, the enterprise will be doomed, and further encouragement would amount to irresponsible cruelty.

One of the sturdier pillars supporting the mystique of 'psychodynamic' therapies is the notion that therapeutic change, if it is to be accounted valid, has to be an outcome of the therapy itself, an aspect of the alchemical reaction which supposedly takes place in the crucible of the 'therapeutic relationship'. In fact, however, exactly the opposite seems to me to be the case. Whatever the temporary enthusiasms which may be fired in people through solidarity with a counsellor or therapist, the world will inexorably reassert its grip unless they can marshal against it powers and resources which are in themselves thoroughly mundane. Changing (or finding) jobs, moving house, forming new bonds or associations with others, acquiring knowledge or abilities which can be put to use in changing one's circumstances:

these are the kinds of events and activities which make a real difference to the way that people feel. (Perhaps what misled traditional theorists was that so many of their clients already possessed a wide range of such resources, so that the most visibly significant change appeared to be a therapeutically inspired 'decision' to deploy them in new ways.)

For the person whose troubles are caused most fundamentally by events or difficulties in the present, the possession of appropriate powers and resources is a hopeful indication that they may be able to resolve them. If you have the money and the requisite vocational abilities and qualifications, you can, for example, change your job or your location. If you have the money and the brains, you can equip yourself with new abilities through further training or education. If you are not too old, too unattractive or too inextricably materially enmeshed in current relationships, you may be able to form new ones. If you have none of these powers and resources, you will be entirely at the mercy of a world which is quite likely to turn out to be a ruthlessly cruel one.

Change, in short, comes about through somebody being able physically and materially to alter their *position* in the world, to escape malign influences or to find benign ones. The motive power for making such moves is *always* either directly or indirectly traceable to resources which are or have historically been (for example, in the form of education) acquired from outside. The ultimate 'therapy' is thus the acquisition of some kind of socioeconomic advantage, and it is above all this fact which the psychotherapies have helped so effectively to mystify.

Therapists may be therapeutic to the extent that they can help people identify the powers and resources needed to tackle their difficulties and encourage them where possible to acquire them. In this respect therapy is much more like teaching than the esoteric enterprise it is so often made out to be, but with the unfortunate difference that the arts to be taught and the manner of teaching them are not specified. In most cases, then, the therapist is reduced to making fairly obvious suggestions about how patients might tackle things – for example, by joining an evening class, making new social contacts, seeking legal advice about difficult domestic situations, etc. In one form or another this kind of encouragement usually consists of helping people to extend their own influence upon their lives beyond the most immediately proximal sphere in which they *feel* their miseries into the slightly more distal regions where the *mediation* of them may be modified a little. The details of how such changes may be made are left largely to trial and error, and therapeutic expertise falls a long way short of actually being able to offer people a step–by–step blueprint of how to make life more comfortable.

There are, of course, particular times in people's lives when the possibility of change – the opportunity actually to take up a new stance in the world – is greater than at others. Adolescence is one such period. It seems likely that therapeutic encouragement given at a time when the individual has the opportunity to act upon it will be much more powerful than when there is virtually no room for manoeuvre. Society, so to speak, 'licenses' the adolescent to escape one powerful set of influences before becoming too deeply enmeshed in another, and knowledgeable and considered advice at this point in someone's life may be extremely important and useful. In the same way some forms of activity are much more permissible at one stage as compared with another. It is, for example, entirely respectable for a child to be learning to read and write, but far less so for an adult – it usually takes a lot of courage for someone to go to adult literacy classes. For these reasons it is important for anyone in a helping role both to be aware of the 'windows of opportunity' which life offers people for change, and to try, through the process of encouragement, to help force them open a little where they are shut.

There may also be some value in therapists offering their clients solidarity and encouragement in the face of unfamiliarity. Most therapists will have encountered people's frequent reluctance to make important changes to their lives even when they have the necessary resources to do so. Usually this is because the making of such changes would require their entering frighteningly unfamiliar territory. So rather than making what seems to be an obviously necessary and easily possible change, people may persist in an unproductive and perhaps damaging form of conduct which, even if it once served them well enough, has long since ceased to do so.

Mystified by psychoanalysis as 'repetition compulsion', this kind of difficulty seems to have much more to do with the virtually universal adult preference for familiarity. Apart from anything else, one is not socially 'licensed' as an adult to experiment with ways of relating to people or to display obvious uncertainty or idiosyncrasy in one's dealings with them. What may seem charming in a child may well be extremely strange or even offensive in an adult, and once people have learned the lessons of their youth, they are not only understandably reluctant to abandon them, but there may well be real difficulty in the social acceptability of their doing so.

Rather than therapists imputing such difficulties to some kind of neurotic failure of development, it would be more helpful for them to deliberate over the construction of a theory and practice which reflected more truthfully the realities of their position. Though this would destroy much of their mystique, it might also affirm their role as accomplices and encouragers of people who, though in possession of the necessary resources, lack the support to embark on an arduous course of learning and to take real social risks in the process of making changes to the circumstances of their lives.

The activities of comforting, clarifying and encouraging are not in themselves in any way dishonourable. Indeed, these have always been the ingredients of any effective kind of proximal help, whether given formally by doctors, priests and psychotherapists, or informally by friends and families. If we ceased to be able to perform these functions for each other life would become unbearable, even though in performing them we may make only the shallowest impression on the past and present environmental influences which cause our distress. When we come to confront the reasons for our distress, then, the 'therapeutic' functions are both highly essential and completely inadequate, and this is because on the one hand they touch us in the proximal sphere in which our lives are lived, experienced and felt, and on the other because they are incapable of reaching out into the distal regions where lie the origins of our social ills.

I do not agree with those radical critiques of psychotherapy which condemn it because of the involvement in the therapeutic relationship of an imbalance of power. I noted in Chapter Two how in some ways the unusual power structure of the therapeutic situation is what gives it what little advantage it may have over informal helping relations (for example, the rule that one person talks while the other listens). Power is not in itself immoral; indeed no good could be done without it. The power of loving adults is essential to the proper development of children. We shall not overcome the difficulties of our social environment by abdicating from positions of power.

What makes psychological forms of help suspect is not so much the relative power of their practitioners as the falsity of the claims they so often make, along with the paucity of their concepts and the ineffectiveness of their procedures. In exploiting magical thinking they obscure our vision of the reasons for our difficulties and sap our determination to take on the rigours of trying to change them; in assuming a technical guise they conceal their ignorance of any truly effective method while illicitly appropriating forms of help which belong to everyone.

It can be argued, I think very persuasively (as Jeffrey Masson has done), that because any effective and justifiable form of psychotherapy is nothing more than a human undertaking, a form of moral conduct which *in principle* cannot be technicized or taught, it cannot be legitimately given the status of *profession*. Certainly there is nothing in the procedures of psychotherapy, in the forms in which comfort, clarification and encouragement can be offered, which cannot be – and indeed should not be – done by anyone. I think, however, that it is possible for people to acquire a degree of expertise by virtue of becoming familiar with particular kinds of difficulty or distress through lengthy acquaintance with them. Knowledge comes from experience, and it is certainly likely that a practitioner who has encountered particular kinds of problems in a wide range of instances may learn more useful ways of helping than someone who is new to them.

In this respect 'therapy' and 'counselling' are not – as they are so often made out to be – 'skills' in themselves which can be applied to any form of distress which comes along (any more than 'music' is a 'skill' which can be applied to the playing of any instrument you care to name). Far from being a contentless 'skill', effective help is likely always to be part and parcel of a *knowledge* of the kinds of difficulty to be tackled. But knowledge, of course, is precisely what is in shortest supply in the psychological therapies.

Knowledge may be either transmitted or exploited. The great danger in the professionalization of help in the form of 'therapy' is that it hugs what little it knows to itself for commercial gain, rather than passing it on to its clients. Such knowledge may be used to disparage others for their ignorance while they are kept dependent on the knower for its fruits.

Disparagement, certainly, is a feature of the psychiatric and psychological literature. It is extremely difficult to think of any major text in these fields which does not either belittle those who become the objects of its attention, or patronize them by holding before them an ideal of how they ought to be. At the same time, there is, of course, absolutely nothing to justify such professional conceit – no evidence that the authors of such texts know better than anyone else how to live their lives, and none that the application of their methods actually leads to a significant amelioration of distress.

The clinical gaze which sorts and labels those it falls upon into various categories of inadequacy and incompetence, the professional hubris which presumes to know how unhappy people should 'adjust' themselves to their fate, are surely in need of the humility which would come from the recognition that their claims are bogus and their methods bankrupt. Our gaze needs rather to turn out towards the world in a sober appreciation of the infinity of ways in which social forces over which we have no control throw our lives into chaos and generate ever new and intractable varieties of pain.

Psychologists, psychiatrists and psychotherapists – the police force of 'normality' – need to switch their focus from the physical and mental 'interiors' of their patients to stand with them in human solidarity while together they probe the social space around them for the causes of our distress. We surely have by now abundant evidence that nobody knows how people should be, and if they do are incapable of conveying it. The most we can hope to know is how to reduce some of the impact of some painful influences, and this is done by helpfully taking people's sides, not by diagnosing or by lecturing them.

In our private aspect – that part of our personal experience which is not knitted into or given shape by the social 'forms' we share – we are *all* lonely, eccentric and bizarre. As far as we can be, we need to be supported in our idiosyncrasy and reassured that we are not alone in loneliness; we need, that is, an informed understanding of what it is to be human, to have spent our lives located bodily in a position which *nobody* else can share in a world which, potentially, *everybody* else shares. We do not need our imagination to be policed and our feelings to be regulated by moralizing professionals who are no less victims than we of the ruthless forces which too often make our lives so bitter and our hopes so blighted. We need to be seen as characters whose experience of the world, however bizarre, gives us something true to say about it, and something which might usefully be heeded by others. We have nothing to thank those people for who seek in one way or another to pass judgement on the validity of our experience. Our pain is not an indication of what is the matter with us, but of something which is hurting us from outside.

It is sometimes helpful to suggest to people that, rather than thinking of themselves as social inadequates in need of adjustment, as containers of various undesirable components, they consider themselves as they would a character in a novel: as individual, certainly, but as interesting, as signifying something about the world and as having something to say about it. Nobody really expects characters in novels to get themselves sorted out and 'normalized' in psychotherapy. One seeks to *understand* and *appreciate* characters rather than to change them. To the extent that fiction is less inclined to look for magical solutions to the 'problems' set by its characters, it is more 'real' than life.

Many of the people whose distress drives them to consult a professional expert of some kind do so because they are afraid or ashamed of feeling what they feel, seeing what they see or being who they are. It may help them a little to be taken seriously and to discover thereby that their experience has meanings which point out beyond themselves to a complex and difficult world which none of us knows how to handle. Often it will transpire that they have already done all that they could with exemplary courage and concern for others, but for one reason or another have been unable to give themselves (or get from others) much credit for their efforts. For the most part it's not they who need changing, but the world.

CHAPTER SIX

A Rational Faith

The confusion and distress which form so intractable a part of so many people's lives at this time, and which are so often mistakenly ascribed to an 'interior', personal failure, in fact originate in two main varieties of distal influence. The first, described in detail in Chapter Four, stems from the socio-economic pressures of big business. Its effects (on the vast majority who do not profit from it) are oppressive, painful and acutely unsettling. Radical insecurity is its chief characteristic, and it is profoundly inimical to all those forms of activity which show human beings in their best, most productive and constructive light. The conditions which permit peaceful collaboration, concentrated, creative work and disinterested intellectual enquiry are instantly destroyed by insecurity and threat, which create in their place strife, competitiveness, callousness and fear.

The second main variety of distal influence might better be described as a lack of influence: the breakdown of 'form'. The collapse of traditional systems of values, the tendency to individualization induced by market pressures, the disintegration of the public sphere, the privatization of morals, have all been remarked upon by those who sense the gathering of a millennial crisis the outcome of which is completely incalculable. However this may turn out to be on the grand scale, there is no doubt about its effects on the experience of individuals.

In that proximal sphere in which we are fated to live our lives, the *rules* by which we may do so are no longer clear. The only easily identifiable rules that there are – those of the market – are either simply not adequate or positively inappropriate as guides to social and ethical living.

To take perhaps the most obvious example, the extent of the guidance they give on how men and women should conduct their relations with each other – as competitors, exploitable objects of satisfaction, replaceable commodities, etc. – just does not take account of the problems set by being embodied in a world from which, however hard you try, gender cannot easily be eradicated. And so, lacking 'forms' which enter, *as part of their personhood*, into the structuring of their lives, people experience confusion, bewilderment, self-doubt and suspicion. We don't know how to 'go on' any more not because we lack the intelligence or will to live decently and sociably, but because the necessary guidelines for doing so have disappeared.

And they have disappeared for good reasons. I am not about to make a plea for the return of 'Victorian values' (not least because that is in large measure exactly what in the eighties we got), but want rather to point out that it is precisely the unsatisfactoriness of old values which makes any return to previous, apparently more settled times impossible. From the oppressive domination of a corrupt Church to the hypocritical imposition of the suffocating, conformist values of European imperialism, from the stupid pomposity of privilege to the terror-inducing rhetoric of Stalinism, there has one way and another been a long history of life-destroying 'moralities' imposed on ordinary people by systematic power. There seems absolutely no reason to believe that Business Culture has done any better.

Small wonder that power in any shape or form has been and is being radically called into question by those sensitive to the pain it has so consistently inflicted. From the measured, intellectually and ethically often very attractive speculations of eighteenth- and nineteenth-century anarchists (William Godwin, Alexander Herzen, Peter Kropotkin, Proudhon, Leon Tolstoy), through the reflections of social critics of twentieth-century American society (Paul Goodman, Murray Bookchin, Christopher

Lasch, Noam Chomsky), to the protestations of the oppressed minorities of the present time (the familiar triad of gays, blacks and women), the question arises as to whether *any* form of power which creates and enforces social rules can be morally viable and acceptable.

The greatest of all critics of power, Michel Foucault, seemed to see power as inseparable from a technology of normalizing rules, and yet there is more than a hint in the developments of most recent times that power may manifest itself in an unexpected guise – that of, precisely, the *absence* of rules. For with the 'triumph' of capitalism and the 'end of history' proclaimed by the euphoric wing of 'postmodernity', it seems that the society held together by the discipline of scientific surveillance which Foucault so brilliantly revealed is metamorphosing into one which thrives upon the superficial anarchism created by deregulation and 'blue-sky' make-believe. Disciplinary scientism is being replaced by magical liberalism, but both are equally the creation of power.

For power is not synonymous with rules. Power will employ *any* strategy which creates privilege, distinction and advantage. Anything at all which results in the accretion of economic and ideological control will be adapted and adopted by power. A mistake of systematic thinking about social and cultural issues has often been to underestimate the resourcefulness and adaptability of power, which is as resourceful and adaptable as human ingenuity can make it. Marx may well have been right about the inherent contradictions of the capitalism of his day, but power can cope with contradictions. If things get too inconveniently contradictory, you just move the goal posts.

Foucault's particular genius was to show how institutions masquerading as caring were really controlling. It may well be, however, that power can, for a while, best maintain its position by abandoning care/control for a chaotic free-for-all in which the privileged are isolated from the teeming, disorganized mass through sheer invisibility as much as anything else. This would be the extreme development of the contrast between a hidden private affluence and an ungoverned and all too obvious public squalor.

Absence of rules does thus not necessarily bring freedom, and certainly not equality. There are rules and rules: oppressive ones which we would be well rid of, and constructive ones which are the very fabric of our social being. On the whole we have not been very discriminating about which are which.

It has often struck me (as no doubt it has many people) how, for the most part, amazingly well ordered road traffic is. Rush-hour traffic on a busy city ring road, for example, is an extraordinary phenomenon of co-ordination, anticipation and co-operation. All those people of the most varied social condition and personal temperament, with utterly different interests and preoccupations, irreconcilable values, young, old, male and female, all manage to obey the same, quite stringent and tightly defined rules. The odd maverick, it is true, may switch lanes inconsiderately, vehicles may break down, accidents, of course, happen. But given the volume of traffic, the number of people and the complexity of their differing aims in travelling, it is an astonishingly stable and predictable situation. So it certainly is not the case that we cannot and do not willingly conduct ourselves according to rules. What seems to permit us to do so is our being able to appreciate their usefulness and see that they have been constructed in our interest.

But if the Highway Code can command our assent, there seems to be very little, other than 'the market', to organize our conduct on the grander scale, and the absence of a coherent and codifiable moral order is making the experience of living increasingly difficult and painful for larger and larger numbers of people. We have tried an authoritarian God, and that didn't work. We have tried both the majesty of the King and the dictatorship of the proletariat, and they brought us only grief. The project of the Enlightenment – the belief in Reason and Science as the foundation of a golden future – is also widely proclaimed to have failed. Certainly the tyrannical objectivity which became established via a degenerate scientism, even though it still maintains a disciplinary hold on our lives, has become so discredited as to be scarcely any longer viable, and in any case appears to have outlived its usefulness. Aside from Business values, what else seems to be on offer?

Now that the old 'forms' have been exposed as 'grand narratives' which simply couldn't bear the moral weight placed upon them, it is not particularly difficult to identify the ideological influences which compete to take their place. The appeal of fundamentalist religion is particularly in evidence, and seems to offer a rallying point both in societies which offer little hope of material comfort and for sections of affluent Western populations which find the insecurities generated by Business values rather more than they can cope with.

There is clearly a strong element of wishful thinking in the reborn varieties of Christianity which appeal to so many people, but there is nothing like association to give magical wishfulness an appearance of solid reality. The shattering of that part of our personhood which is structured by 'form' is experienced as the kind of pain which cries out to be assuaged by the comfort of association. As a last resort people seem to seek refuge and stability by huddling together on any moral high ground that offers, whether in rigid adherence to 'politically correct' ideologies concerning gender and sexuality, etc., or in the sometimes quite fanatical espousal of surprisingly small-scale moralisms such as vegetarianism, anti-smoking campaigns, and so on.

Nationalism fulfils a function similar to that of fundamentalist religion, but is probably considerably more powerful in view of the ready-made associative strength of nationality. It takes, to put it mildly, quite a stretch of the imagination to believe that Jesus Christ is taking a personal interest in your everyday affairs, but that you are a Serb or a Croat seems simply a matter of fact, and already a sound basis for getting together with other Serbs or Croats. Nothing seems more predictable than that, as other values which give social coherence disappear, nationalism should once again cast its shadows across human society.

If religiosity and patriotism fail to appeal, there is still the option of turning one's back on the public sphere altogether in order to celebrate 'interiority'. Apart from the vulgar privatism of Business, in which the ideal of life is to 'enjoy' both your personal possessions and your commodified 'relationships' in the privacy of your own home, there are the morally rather more sophisticated approaches to life which suggest that its value lies in the cultivation of the self and the riches thought to be contained therein. Whether fostering the 'personal growth' of the humanist psychotherapies, or tending the 'God within' of theologies which, like Don Cupitt's, have 'at last understood that our life has no outside',[1] the emphasis is on the inward-turned gaze which endlessly contemplates selves or souls in order to render them more personally satisfactory.

Apart from such approaches as these, then, we have little to shape our common purpose except the 'magical liberalism' which is loosely and somewhat incoherently associated with Business values. Rules and regulations, other than those of the mediocratically imposed discipline which generates competition and insecurity, are out, and they are out partly because of the further insecurity that their absence occasions. In the place of the old 'grand narratives' of medieval and reformation Christianity and the Enlightenment quest for scientific certainty and ethical confidence, we have a motley collection of petty narratives whose relatedness to material circumstances and wishful thinking is so obvious that there seems little likelihood of their achieving more than some temporarily expedient goal (for example, securing national boundaries or warding off the invasion of personal insecurity).

We are left, in fact, with a 'postmodern' relativity of values or 'narratives' from which, in the best market tradition, you pays your money and takes your choice. I have no doubt at all that this state of affairs gives rise to considerable distress, and I hope

---

1. From the back cover of his *The Long-Legged Fly*, SCM Press, 1987.

that it is by now clear from what has gone before that this is not just a matter of our 'not knowing what to believe in', or of not being provided with some kind of arbitrary moral goal to cement our social life into a common purpose, but is rather a factor of part of our nature as persons having disintegrated. This is, of course, the part of our personhood which is situated in the social environment outside our bodies. Its breakdown is our breakdown because 'we' are not separable from 'it'. But 'it' cannot be reconstructed through an attempted therapeutic reconstruction of our 'selves': if we want to 'feel better' we have to pay direct attention to the reconstruction of that part of our common environment whose disintegration is making us all feel bad in the first place.

At present, our common social environment, where it has not fractured into various essentially magical relativities or nationalistic interest groups, is held together only by the precarious structure given it by Business Culture. If the economic basis upon which that world is built (and whatever one thinks of it, it is at least real) should collapse – as indeed in its present form it surely must – we shall be in a sorry state indeed, with nothing to fall back on but the barbarous attachments dictated largely by our biology.

What we need is not a 'narrative', grand or petty, with which to glue together our fractured social lives, for it is precisely our having seen through such narratives – their arbitrariness and hypocrisy, the smoke screen they have provided for the machinations of power – which has led to their demise. We need rather to *re-establish a relationship with reality* which has all but disappeared into magic and wishful relativities.

For however seduced we may have been by our own inventiveness, by the power of make-believe and the artistry of a huge promotional industry, however dazzled by the endlessly reflecting images of a 'postmodernity' in which it begins to seem that absolutely everything is 'in the mind', it is still the case that we do live in a real world, and more than ever the case that we need to come to a satisfactory accommodation with it.

If the 'project of the Enlightenment' collapsed into the totalitarianism, strife and destruction of the twentieth century, does that really mean that the search for truth, justice and equality which inspired it is discredited, or may it be that it is only the means of trying to attain them which can be shown to have failed?

One of the central messages emerging from the mixture of confusion, despair and excitement which appears to be attending the close of this millennium is that 'form' is passé, that we have nothing to rely upon but our selves and whatever organizing principles can be excavated from their interior spaces. The sober constraints of an 'outside' which, it is felt, is so hopelessly beyond our understanding as to be not worth further serious consideration seem to be giving way to a Nietzschean exultation in a kind of absolute subjectivity which places humankind not merely at the centre of the universe, but practically encompassing it as its container.

But if 'form' is necessary to our integrity as persons, we shall have to continue to pay attention to the nature of the world as its creatures rather than its containers. If the project of the Enlightenment failed to reveal to us a reality solid enough for us to anchor ourselves in reasonably comfortably and harmoniously, it need not mean that we have to abandon the project so much as learn from our mistakes. It is still, I submit, not only relevant, but more than ever essential to pursue two fundamental Enlightenment questions: what is it possible to believe and what is it right to do?

The point of pursuing these questions – knowledge and truth on the one hand and ethical guidance on the other – is not simply to keep academics in business (allowing the intellectual market to corner these concerns is precisely one of the mistakes we have made in the past) but to reconstruct an essential pole of our personhood by placing ourselves in a viable relationship to the real world we actually do live in and which we absolutely cannot wish away.

KNOWLEDGE AND TRUTH

The concept of 'truth' and the forms of knowledge which have been built upon its foundations have not been unsullied by the interests of power. Indeed, far from being the shining centre of enlightened humanity's quest for liberation, truth is quickly turned into a blunt instrument of oppression. Rather than providing the gateway to an understanding we can joyfully pursue together, truth becomes the brutal, cruelly unresisting fact which whips your arms behind your back and marches you helplessly along the narrow paths laid down by those who 'know'.

It is quite remarkable how politicians, when they are about to lie most blatantly, preface their utterance with 'the truth is . . .' The truth they invoke is the truth which constrains the opposition and shuts up objectors, the same truth to whose demands generations of school children have been terrorized into trying to conform, the truth which paralyses dissent and exacts obedience.

The truth pursued in scientific knowledge, most clearly evident in the wonderful intellectual liberation of those courageous seekers who fought their way free of the grim discipline of the Church, soon enough became yet another form of that discipline, this time embodied in the dogmas of logical positivists and other systematic thinkers who like to set rules for what it is possible to believe.

It is really quite difficult for most people even to imagine a concept of 'truth' which is not tied so closely into some kind of discipline as to be more or less identical with it. Truth is what we *have to* believe and what we cannot escape from, either because it is defined and laid down by some absolute Authority or because it is stamped with an equally absolute Objectivity which cannot be gainsaid. Truth, for most people, is either to be possessed or feared as a weapon for controlling or being controlled by others. As an instrument of power, its availability becomes strictly limited, and inevitably it ends up embedded in a whole technology of secrecy. Truth is dangerous.

It is also extremely difficult for most of us to disconnect the idea of truth from that of certainty. What gives it such invincible authority, what makes it such a prized commodity and such a dangerous weapon is its infallibility. Truth is the final arbiter, and before its judgement one can only stand in dumb submission. Philosophers who have been concerned to duck from under the tyranny of one form of 'infallible' truth have nearly always sought to establish another in its place by discovering something new which cannot be doubted (something, naturally, which suited them more than those they saw as their intellectual oppressors). And as soon as a suitable candidate is found for the role of indubitable instrument of liberation, it is immediately appropriated by power as the next weapon of oppression. The science which slew God becomes the all-pervasive net of discipline in which Foucault showed us we are caught.

The same fate is sure to await the efforts of those who seek to replace 'truth' by an entirely new authority which repudiates its ancient claims altogether. There have since Nietzsche been various attempts at suggesting that there *is* no truth, no grounds of certainty, but only our own desire and will, nothing but infinite relativities of perspective, so that ultimately only might determines right. From critics of 'modernity' (like Herbert Marcuse) who have suggested that we may escape to freedom via an unbridled eroticism, to apologists of 'postmodernity' who (like Richard Rorty) frankly make pragmatic self-interest the foundation of our concerns, there has been a great deal of intellectual activity in recent decades aimed no doubt at undermining the despotic claims of certain 'truth'. But there is no revolutionary thought here which cannot be comfortably adapted by power.

It seems strange at first that the compound of Reason and Power which we discover 'truth' to have been made of should be considered by so many present-day thinkers to have been rendered more liberating by dissolving from it the element of Reason. But strange only so long as we forget that those thinkers cannot avoid living in and being shaped by a world which is itself structured by power. If power can operate successfully by dropping its

pretence of reason, why shouldn't it do so? As long as 'truth' had
the authority of certainty, it was needed by power to underwrite
its claims about the nature of the 'real world', but once certainty
has been shown to be a philosophical impossibility, truth (which
in any case carried with it many inconvenient limitations on
power's freedom to do *exactly* what it liked) can be discarded as
a rather out-moded and uncomfortable old garment.

An interesting characteristic of the 'old' concept of truth as
indubitable knowledge, as the certain ground of what we may
believe, is the extent to which it is suffused with magic: a longing
for absolute knowledge-power which will give us absolute control.
It does indeed seem to be the case that philosophers who pursued
the infallible ground of truth were as ludicrously mistaken as
tormented alchemists trying to distil gold from base metals. The
most powerful lesson taught us by science itself is that there can
be no ultimate certainty.

But rather than drawing from this the 'postmodern' conclusion
that knowledge based on truth must be abandoned, that truth
is after all a useless concept, could we not rather see that what
is needed is to receive gratefully a concept of truth divested of
magic and to elaborate it in the sober realization that though it
will not yield up to us absolute power, it is nevertheless the best
tool we have for understanding our world? Having arrived at the
possibility of separating Reason from Power, should we not
explore the nature of Reason a little further before we give
ourselves over totally to be enveloped in unmitigated Power?

At first, to be sure, we may be a little disorientated, for if truth
based on reason has no ground in a certain authority, what possible
use could it be to us – what, for instance, would make it different
from opinion or guesswork? But the answers to questions such
as these are, in fact, already quite easily available in scientific
thought, and indeed the practice of reason is quite familiar from
everyday experiences.

Scientific enquiry proceeds in the recognition that all it ever
establishes conclusively is that something is not the case, never

that 'the truth' has finally been arrived at. What even scientists themselves have not always seen is that the lesson to be learned from this is not that 'the truth' must for ever elude their grasp, but that there is literally no such kind of 'truth' as this: it is an unattainable, magical ideal. So far as 'truth' has any meaning (and, of course, it does), it lies precisely in what scientists do: that is, in trying to establish that one is not mistaken, that one is not making a claim which can be shown to be false by someone who examines the evidence and arguments more closely and carefully. There is no *ultimate* truth waiting in the wings to pop out one triumphant day and put its seal of approval on our speculations. But this does not have to mean that 'anything goes', that we can think anything we like, or that if you make enough people agree with you by main force you have as good as arrived at 'the truth'.

The truth exists precisely in its separation from the constraints of power. The truth is what we arrive at when we have the freedom and resources to look for it. There *is* no truth beyond that truth. Although, of course, the scientific community can quite easily become colonized by power so that its principles and practices are hardened into disciplinary dogmatisms (this has certainly happened in the social sciences), ideally scientific practice is characterized precisely by the freedom of its community to pursue it. There are, of course, always dangers – particularly apparent once again at the present time – that scientific knowledge will be appropriated into whatever constitutes the current 'discourse of power'. In this way Business, as it takes over universities and removes the protections of academic freedom, threatens to reduce scientific enquiry to sterile technological routines which merely exploit applications of what is known rather than seek to know.

Scientific knowledge is by no means the only kind which pursues truth in ways which are at least potentially disengaged from the oppressive interests of power. Reason is liberated by the absence of threat. Any situation which removes from people the possibility of their being punished for what they think allows them to investigate their world with the kind of dedicated seriousness which displays rationality at its most admirable. This may sometimes happen, for example, in individual or group psychotherapy where the judgemental attitudes which literally constitute our ordinary social activity may be temporarily lifted. It may also happen as a jury tries in good faith and without prejudice to determine the weight to be given the evidence it has heard.

Reason is, of course, not completely detachable from power. To operate effectively it needs access to the resources which fuel its exercise. Even in the absence of threat, the individual's untutored perspective is not on its own sufficient to guarantee a reasonable judgement or true belief. The reasoned pursuit of truth is a communal activity, calling upon the collaboration of others in enterprises which may well span generations. Just as 'truth' is not a commodity which may be individually appropriated and wielded as a weapon, but rather the ever-corrigible judgement of a society, so knowledge can only be pursued in an unconstrained association with others who seek to establish no patent on what they find.

One of the strongest currents in the philosophical tradition concerned with knowledge and truth has tended to suggest that if we cannot say with certainty what the nature of the world is, we must have imagined it. If the world isn't so insistently 'real' that we are all ultimately stunned by the sheer weight of the evidence into acknowledging what it is like, then it must simply consist of ideas in our heads, and anyone's idea is probably as good as anyone else's.

In many ways this realist/idealist debate is reflected in the issue of exteriority/interiority which has been such a bone of contention in psychology, and indeed a central preoccupation of this book. But the philosophical version of 'interiority' is writ very much larger than the psychological one: it is not merely suggesting that there are such things as interior worlds, but that the world itself is interior. The argument implied (though, of course, not stated anything like as crassly as this) seems to run along the lines that if we cannot describe reality in complete and convincing detail (sufficiently incontrovertibly as to be able to beat doubters into submission with 'the truth'), we might as well give up the whole idea and let ourselves rip with the various imaginary versions which we can create out of our own desires, interests and impulses. If 'reality' is not our master, we might as well make it the plaything of our fantasy.

The fallacy of this kind of thinking stems from the essentially magical conviction that if there is 'a reality' we must be able to say with certainty what 'it' is (and that, therefore, if we cannot say what 'it' is, there cannot be one). All this tells us really is that human beings have an overwhelming need to achieve intellectual certainty and an extraordinarily inflated belief in the significance of their own mental productions. There is something remarkably infantile about this. Even if we have grown up enough to recognize that we have to do without a benign and omnipotent God, perhaps we now have further to realize that 'truth' in the form of certain knowledge is also irretrievably beyond our grasp.

There are some interesting, and strangely paradoxical, parallels between our attitude to knowledge and our attitude to religion. Most of us would probably feel that, while religion is the arena of our beliefs and superstitions, which can lay no claim to objective validity, secular or scientific knowledge is testable against a reality which can be known. In fact, however, something close to the contrary is arguable: it is precisely *from* religion that we have taken over and projected into secular knowledge our infantile yearning for certainty. While we may have given up God, we have not given up the concept of 'Truth' on which religious awe and obedience were founded. Indeed, 'science' seemed to offer a safer home for that concept than did the Church. Even more paradoxically, what we now need to recognize is that, to recover a usable concept of truth, we have to reconnect 'science' with the idea of *uncertain* belief, or faith. It thus becomes *more* scientific to *believe*, or have *faith* in the reality of our world, than it does to have 'certain knowledge' of it.

There seems to me no contradiction in saying that the nature of reality is a mystery which can *never* be known with any certainty, but about which we should always try to speak the truth. Even though this contention runs superficially counter to some of our less reflective everyday thinking, it nevertheless does nothing more than state the obvious. Reality *is* a mystery to us, but the fact that we can only know it from our own perspectives and for our own purposes does not mean that it is not 'there'. We all have a sense of its being 'there', and in our everyday lives we, wisely, treat its presence with considerable respect: we don't try to walk through brick walls or fly unaided by machinery over chasms. We seek to avoid pain and we know how to inflict it. We are in no fundamental doubt about the reality of the world in which we find ourselves. Why, then, not try in good faith to develop together a knowledge of what we are in no fundamental doubt about? Why not try to tell each other the truth about our experiences as creatures embodied in a natural and social environment? The fact that in doing so we are necessarily unable to arrive at an ultimate description of the universe which fixes its character for all time and brooks no alternative perspective is absolutely no cause for despair. The proof that we can do this perfectly successfully is, once again, that that is precisely what, at its best, scientific enquiry does do (even if it is not often encountered at its best).

There is no reason why our being unable to demonstrate with complete conviction 'what reality is' should cause us to lose our nerve and deny its relevance and validity altogether. We need only recognize the magical absurdity of *trying* to say 'what it is', and take up a position of relatively unruffled belief in its significance as it manifests itself to us.

We need to do this as much as anything in order to regain a purchase upon the world which has become dangerously loose. Both through our rigid insistence on particular dogmatic versions of 'reality' ('certain truth') and through our more recent tendency to slide into self-interested relativities which scoff at the idea of truth of any kind, we have become prey to manipulations of our world by forms of oppressive power which we are barely able to recognize, let alone control.

We need to rediscover procedures of enquiry and a conceptual language which enable us truly to describe what is happening to us, and to build 'forms' for our experience which are, precisely, rooted in reality and able to receive the assent, *freely given*, of the communities they help to shape. Rather than being browbeaten into accepting versions of 'the truth' which come in the end to be exposed as the hypocritical mythologies of a self-serving structure of power, we need to *discover* the important features of the social *reality* which encompasses us and gives form and content to our experience. We need to be able to describe the world which makes us feel as we do, and to describe it accurately. We have to clarify together the nature of our predicament.

As always, it is much easier to see what is needed than to be able to say how to achieve it. In fact, there probably is no recipe for the reconstruction of society, even though we can see what makes it, as it is, so psychologically damaging, and even though we can specify some of the conceptual changes to our ways of thinking about the world which would be necessary to our making of it a more comfortable habitat. Societies are not made like cakes, and even though clubs of intellectuals and social engineers (like, for example, the Adam Smith Institute) may have their day, their contribution to giving shape to the times is probably far less significant than they think. The vast network of interest which holds our social environment in place is extremely unlikely to be moved by an idea, or even by several ideas mooted in concert; it is much more the case that the network itself generates the ideas which oppose as well as support it. But that is the point: 'the system' is not infallible, and where it gives rise to injustice and pain, it risks being modified by its own negative consequences.

The aim of suggesting procedures for the reconstruction of 'form', and of developing what are in the end philosophical conceptions to help with that process, is not to provide a recipe for social revolution which will strike into the hearts of the oppressed and bring them out into the streets. It is rather to try to clarify issues in ways which may help people diagnose the nature of their predicament and encourage them to take advantage of whatever opportunities may present themselves for improving things.

It should I hope by now be clear that the 'reconstruction of "form" ', even though it raises philosophical issues concerning truth and knowledge which are rarely seen as the concern of 'ordinary people', is not just an arid intellectual game. I have already suggested that a concept of truth sufficiently viable to enable us to describe our common world – the reality in which we find ourselves – in ways to which we can give our assent cannot be developed outside a certain kind of context. This context must be free of threat, must contain other people in an association of good faith, and must have access to the kinds of resources which make such enquiry possible (the tools of education, and so on).

It is not always the case that intellectual activity is seen as dependent on requirements of this kind (though there are eminent thinkers who suggest that it is – in particular Jürgen Habermas). What underlies these requirements is in essence an *ethical* position. In the division of labour which characterizes universities as much as any other institution, 'ethics' has tended as a discipline to be split off from 'epistemology' (theory of knowledge), as if the one had very little significance for the other. This is rather similar to the split noted above between 'knowledge' and 'faith', and just as we need to knit the latter two concepts together again, so, I think, do we need to see that no purely intellectual enquiry is possible, but that any such enquiry must always be guided by a practical ethics. We cannot really consider what it is possible to believe without thinking also about what it is right to do.

This is especially the case in a situation like ours, where we have to do without certain knowledge as our guide. No doubt if 'truth' were revealed to us (by God, or Objectivity, or some other Authority) as absolute, we might not have to worry too much about how to take it, as we would presumably have little choice. However, if we are, as I have suggested, caught up in a reality whose nature is and will remain essentially mysterious to us, the ways in which we conduct ourselves towards it become problematic. We shall need, in fact, our forms of knowledge to be guided by our ethics, and our ethics to be informed in turn by what we know: the two become inseparable.

ETHICAL GUIDANCE

Moral philosophers have tended to be as preoccupied as their epistemologist colleagues with looking for a form of authority which would establish absolute certainty for their field of enquiry. Just as we long to discover truths which may be known for certain, so we scan the horizon for values which may be held with absolute, unquestioning confidence. We want to know the rules, and we don't want to have to think about them.

In the field of ethics, however, the search for certainty has been even less fruitful than has been the case with nonmoral knowledge. Trying to stipulate rules for right conduct by deriving them from some kind of behavioural formula, or offering a calculus for defining 'good', has always ended in incoherence. Such approaches either commit what the philosopher G. E. Moore called 'the naturalistic fallacy' or leave such obvious gaps and implied contradictions that they are useless as any form of ethical guide.

The 'naturalistic fallacy' points out that any definition of 'good' which is not simply circular – i.e., which does not define 'good' in terms of a disguised synonym of it – always leaves it open to a doubter to question whether what 'good' is said to be *really is* good. There seems, in other words, to be something irreducible about moral concepts such as 'good' which cannot be unpacked into more factual, nonmoral equivalents. Another way of putting this is to point out, as did David Hume, that an 'ought' cannot be derived from an 'is'. One can always ask of a factual state of affairs whether it is right: it is never so self-evidently right as to be capable of providing a *criterion* of rightness.

Attempts at ignoring these difficulties and pressing on regardless have not met with great success. For example, the Utilitarian idea that what is good is what brings the greatest happiness to the greatest number (apart from providing the ideology underpinning the kind of soulless moralism Dickens attacks so effectively in *Hard Times*) soon runs into all kinds of impossible complications. The resulting frustration has left moral philosophers with a limited range of options. One is to suggest that moral judgements are really no more than expressions of personal preference. In the dry language of logical positivism, for example, 'X is good' is taken to be an essentially meaningless statement more or less equivalent, as A. J. Ayer suggested, to 'hurrah for X!'

This is by now a familiar situation: if a basis for our ethical judgement cannot be either found in the absolute authority of God or derived from the incontrovertible nature of a self-revealing Reality, then we have apparently to conclude that it resides somewhere inside ourselves as, for example, a feeling or an impulse which can be no more objectively justifiable than a liking for a particular food.

More recently, it is true, there have been efforts to locate the source of our moral sentiment in the *community* rather than in the *self* (see for example Alasdair MacIntyre's *After Virtue*), but even here there are uneasy questions to be asked about *which* communities may be taken as forging the core structure of a moral system. Once again, with views such as this, we face the possibility that right will be determined by might, and that if you happen to find yourself in the wrong community you may be branded as outside the pale of human values.

Insofar as ethics are all about the way we conduct ourselves towards each other, it certainly seems an advance on some positions to suggest that they should be viewed from the perspective of community. What binds together the individuals who form a community, however, is the part of their personhood which they have in common and which may in large part consist precisely of ethical 'forms'. Certainly communities *will* differ from each other in this respect, as for example Iranian Muslim fundamentalists compared with born-again Christians from the USA. Far from being a cause for moral celebration, this looks more like a recipe for disaster, especially when one considers that 'community' of this kind may be but a large-scale version of an infinity of factions, interest groups and cliques seeking to assert the supremacy of the values they happen to share. Is there no more fundamental basis to a common human morality than (to mention but a few) the political, religious, national, class, race and gender issues which some of us share with others?

To locate the 'forms' of morality in that part of our being which is *cultural* is precisely to 'communitize' humankind in accordance with the religious and national clubs into which it is split, and hence to invite competition and strife into the very core of our ethical outlook. But, even if it is understood very differently by different cultural groups, there *is* something that we *all* share and which provides the foundation for a *general* human community: our existence in the world as embodied subjects.

Psychologists and others, particularly those interested in the simulation of human thought and behaviour by machines, often set themselves the conundrum of trying to define the essential properties of 'humanness'. If a robot could be built that looked, sounded and acted exactly like a person, could it meaningfully be said not to be one? This seems to me a contrived and not really very significant puzzle. What makes us human is our embodiedness: the fact that we possess bodies which are in all essentials identical to each other. An experienced surgeon cutting open any one of us will not be surprised by what is revealed, and if it turned out to be a collection of printed circuits, cables and transistors, would have no difficulty in concluding that it was not a human being under the knife.

The ultimate solidarity is the solidarity of pain. Strip people of power, strip them of all those cultural aspects which give them distinction and individuality – so that they are, indeed, stripped of their very 'personality' – and you are still left with a sentient body, even if one incapable of the functions we normally expect of persons.

It is certainly this solidarity-as-bodies that we recognize and acknowledge in caring for the infirm, the old and the handicapped, who are indeed often deprived of some of the powers which contribute to personhood. It is this solidarity which makes us wince and squirm with sympathetic sensation when we see someone else incur a painful injury. We recognize that, as bodies, we are not distinguishable from each other. It is perhaps also this solidarity which makes it possible for a tiny infant to imitate apparently without trying the exaggerated facial expressions of a parent. So similar are we, we can almost feel each other's feelings, and quite often literally do.

Our vulnerability to pain and our recognition of it in others is what binds us across otherwise unbridgeable divides. The image of the dying body of a Somalian child, leaving a pathetic smear of blood on the pavement as someone gently drags it away by the heels, moves – even though impotently – the comfortable Westerner eating a bag of crisps in front of the television. The discrepancy in power and privilege between these two figures is, to be sure, obscene, and, of course, testifies to a global society which has gone terribly wrong, but nevertheless as long as one is moved by the plight of the other, there must be hope.

It is, of course a truism that people embattled against a common enemy, or otherwise fallen on hard times, may co-operate together in forms of solidarity which completely evaporate in more comfortable circumstances. It is often observed that people living in conditions of Third World poverty seem able to be happy in ways apparently not possible in the affluent West, and certainly anyone who has worked with the underprivileged, the sick and the disabled will know how heroically altruistic people in the worst of all possible worlds can be, and what warmth, support and loving self-sacrifice they can be capable of. It seems that, in some circumstances at least, the more people are reduced to the status of suffering bodies, the more they are able to act with and for each other in a quintessentially moral way.

Perhaps it would be the case that, if we were able to live out our lives in proximal relation to each other, undisturbed by the insecurity and competitiveness imposed by distal influences, our embodied solidarity would provide a basis for genuine community. As things are, however, such a possibility does not arise, and it is only ever the case that we are *forced* into such proximal collaboration by malign distal powers which (like war) are too pervasive in their impact to allow the operation of distinction between those affected – competition is *suppressed* by threat rather than made unnecessary by the absence of threat.

For, except in those cases where threat is so overwhelming as to force a kind of solidarity, power's ultimate resort is to reach right into the body in order to sow the seeds of distinction in this last bastion of community. To exploit the difference between male and female (rather than celebrate its mystery), to invent and accentuate 'racial' issues, to valorize the body in terms of its sexual potency and make it the foundation of an industry of pornography, to invest it with symbols of power by any means available – all these are the techniques of a system which, to survive, must find ever new ways of dividing and ruling, objectifying and commodifying. To manufacture physical differences and distinctions which generate shame, insecurity and competition is to distract us from the subjective embodiment which gives us our most fundamental solidarity.

The reaction to this in present-day society is to attempt a magical disembodiment. The response to the colonization of the body's materiality by power seems to be to deny that the body has any materiality at all. If power succeeds, as undoubtedly it has, in pitting men against women, the response is to assert that there is no difference between men and women. The same is the case with black and white, fat and thin, strong and weak, able and disabled, beautiful and ugly. 'Anorexia' is an expression of the plight of women struggling to free themselves from the curse of having to occupy bodies which have become both biological liabilities and the fetishized objects of a male gaze emptied of all enchantment. The attempted solution of the problem through 'anorexia' is symbolic of a much wider tendency to seek to escape from imprisonment in bodies which are the ultimate target of malign power by denying their existence.

The denial of embodiment, literally in the case of 'anorexia', and by implication in the case of those ideologies which prohibit 'politically incorrect' references to physical characteristics, while understandable and perhaps laudable in intent, is nevertheless profoundly mistaken, and likely to lead to a kind of totalitarian distortion of reality which will only create new punitive moralisms and their attendant repressions. The incoherence of the kind of 'loony left' ideology which prohibits the use of words like 'black' or 'fat' or 'disabled' is that it attempts to combat a malign reality by denying that it can be spoken of. This is similar to the ultimately hopeless anorectic conjuring trick of trying to continue living in a body while starving it out of existence.

Our embodiment is real and inescapably material and does make possible differences and distinctions between us which may be and will be exploited by power. But what is inviolable by power, and what founds our common humanity, is not so much the brute fact of the body's objective materiality as its subjective vulnerability. In the final analysis we all feel the same because we are all constructed in the same way. If you prick us, we bleed. It is *this* which is true whoever you are, and however strong or weak, or beautiful, or rich or important you are.

The appeal which Shakespeare placed in Shylock's mouth is echoed in a moral insight which transcends time, place and culture and which serves to remind us that in the subjective experience of our embodiment we are *not* different from each other.

Tzu-Kung asked, 'Is there a single word which can be a guide throughout one's life?' The Master said, 'It is perhaps the word shu. Do not impose on others what you yourself do not desire.'
Confucius, The Analects, Book XV.

Then one of them, which was a lawyer, asked him . . . Master which is the great commandment in the law? Jesus said unto him Thou shalt love the Lord thy God with all thy heart, and with all thy soul, and with all thy mind. This is the first and great commandment. And the second is like unto it, Thou shalt love thy neighbour as thyself.
Matthew, 22, 35-39

So act that the maxim of your will could always hold at the same time as a principle establishing universal law.
Immanuel Kant, Critique of Practical Reason.

Surely what underlies and unites these three statements, uttered by three very different people for very different reasons and in very different contexts spanning over two millennia, is a recognition that what hurts oneself will hurt others, and vice versa.

It would be unrealistic in the extreme to expect to be able to create a world from which inequality had been banished. It is inconceivable that differences between people and the amounts of power available to them could be eradicated. Although one might hope that in some dimly distant future societies might become established in which power is used more for good than for ill, there seems little doubt that for the time being individuals and groups who have access to power are likely more often than not to use it to maintain their own advantage. This means, in effect, that we cannot expect for the discernible future to live in a social world free of competition, dispute and struggle; equality and justice will have, probably only too literally, to be fought for, and if your more powerful neighbour proves to love himself more than you, you may have, if you are not simply to suffer them passively, forcibly to resist his attentions.

In these circumstances nothing will be gained by *pretending* that everyone is equal or inventing ideologies which proscribe the use of a vocabulary which refers to inequalities which patently do exist. On the other hand, we need to be clear that what makes people unequal is the amount of power they possess or have access to, not some intrinsic quality which somehow becomes attached to their very embodiment.

Perhaps in some semiconscious way nervously aware that *in themselves* they are no different from anyone else, the powerful have often sought to create a myth of personal worth which does indeed extend into their bodies, for example by claiming that 'blue blood' courses through their veins or that 'breeding' is responsible for their refinement and their taste. This can, of course, prove a risky ploy, since if accepted at face value it may backfire as it did in the case of the French aristocracy. Many of the most horrifying excesses of human hatred, in fact, follow from the error of confusing people's power with their embodiment and supposing that you dispose of the former by exterminating the latter.

It may be that underlying the seemingly rather naive Christian advocacy of neighbour-loving, cheek-turning, forgiving others their sins and so on is the insight that it is not another's physical being that threatens you, but only the power he or she possesses. In fact, of course, others seen as threatening may not so much possess power as occupy positions in which they are constrained to mediate it. The prisoner may wish his jailer damned to hell, and could not reasonably be expected to feel otherwise, but in reality the jailer is no less enmeshed in the web of power than the prisoner. To identify evil in the embodiment of the evil-doer is to make a serious mistake, and is one which, of course, the interests of power are happy to have made. There is a danger that any ideological or political movement which implicitly locates wrong-doing or injustice in forms of embodiment actually comes to serve the interests of the very powers it is trying to undo –

varieties of feminism which simply see biological maleness as 'the problem' provide an example.

Once rendered powerless, we are all the same. There is no need to execute the tyrant whose power has been removed, and to do so is merely a pointless cruelty. We need rather to dismantle the structures which make the acquisition of tyrannical power possible (a much more difficult and demanding task). Compassion for each other as embodied beings derives not so much from a sentimental ideal as from a sober acknowledgement of social and biological reality.

Having established that as embodied subjects we are all very much in the same boat, vulnerable to much the same suffering and exposed to similar pains, the conclusion that we should treat others as we would wish to be treated ourselves seems only reasonable. Tragically, as a guide to human conduct, it appears to play little part in the formal, essentially political institutions which structure our society, which for the most part engender and encourage distinction and differentiation. Fundamental solidarity based on our common embodiment tends to be put into practice only informally in the proximal sphere of the lives of the least powerful members of society. Otherwise, it forms a conspicuous part of social practice only in its negative aspect, as a fundamental tenet of torturers and terrorists.

For in a world in which our embodiment is either mystified and exploited by power or the object of a magical denial by those trying to escape from power, it is left exposed to the pitiless devices of those who have calculated its significance only too accurately. While the market promotes a make-believe invulnerability and psychology tells us that salvation is to be found in our mental attitudes, the torturer (by doing unto others what he would most hate having done to him) and the terrorist (who sees that, in our basic equivalence, to injure one is to injure all) make use of ethical truth in the most unscrupulous way imaginable. This looks like a variation on the theme of the devil having all the best tunes.

*

An appreciation of reality which seeks to come to an accommodation with it while acknowledging its ultimate mysteriousness, combined with an ethical solidarity based on the fundamental vulnerability of all people as embodied beings in a social environment structured by power, provides a reasonable enough basis for a clarification of our predicament. It suggests also an *attitude* to people and the world which would be desirable not merely on the grounds of its being 'a good thing' in some charitable but essentially impracticable way, but because caution and common sense would advise it.

Because we cannot know with certainty the nature of the mystery we are caught up in (if, indeed, it has a 'nature'), and because it seems clear that in all basic essentials other people are virtually indistinguishable from ourselves, both we and the reality we find ourselves in need to be approached with respect, humility and care. Having discovered how easily we can mistake our own dreams, fantasies and wishes for ultimate verities which in time disintegrate only too obviously, and frequently catastrophically, we need to construct our knowledge of the world with the utmost circumspection, disturbing it as little as possible in the process in case we do some unforeseen damage.

It is easy to build Utopias in the imagination, and scarcely anyone would deny that the construction of an environment which takes proper account of our embodied vulnerability and seeks to establish a degree of social justice and equality would be a good idea. It is certainly not that we cannot see how to make the world a better place, nor is it the case that we lack the means to do so. So why don't we?

We are, I would suggest, collectively very much in the same position as the individual client of psychotherapy whose predicament has become quite clear, but who still seems strangely incapable of doing anything about it. Why not just apply a bit of will power?

The answer, once again, is that there is no such thing as will power pure and simple. There is inside us no source of moral power which can be called upon at will to shape the material structures of the world. It *feels*, of course, as if there is, but in this case our feelings are misleading. I am not saying that we cannot act upon the world – quite obviously we can, and do. What misleads us into a conception of such action as volitional is that we cannot act without *experiencing* acting, i.e., having a feeling about it, and we take this feeling to be the *cause* of our action, when in fact it is just its necessary accompaniment.

In order to act we need the necessary powers and resources, and the impulse of such power comes most of the time from outside ourselves: we are, so to speak, points in social space *through which* power travels. There are, no doubt, simple acts which we can perform which originate within our biological structure and which we could loosely be said to be able to perform 'at will', but they have little significance: I can scratch my head, or cough, or walk down to the corner shop with the involvement of very little more than my bodily powers. But significant social action requires the contribution of powers considerably more distal than these, and they cannot be willed by me.

The illusion of will rests on the same phenomenon of 'proximality' as do many of the mistakes we make about the causes of our troubles. Any action we take involves our bodily complicity in and commitment to it, and so it is very hard to resist the impression that we are the causes of our actions. What we experience as 'will' is, however, nothing more than the subjective feeling of complicity and commitment in the *transmission* of powers which originate, either currently or in the past, outside us.

Right at the core of the mysteriousness of the reality which surrounds us is the fact that much of the time we cannot, and could not, possibly see what the reasons for our actions are, or what the consequences of them for that reality will be. We *cannot but* act in faith and hope. It is not just that so much happens beyond our power horizon or took place outside the span of our memory, though these factors make understanding difficult enough. It is also the case that, being ourselves part of the world we're trying to understand, we affect it materially in the very act of trying to understand it (Heisenberg's much-cited 'principle of indeterminacy'). So not only is 'free will' essentially illusory, but there is also no possibility of our being able to offer anything like a complete deterministic account of our actions either.

In some senses, this leaves us with little option but to *believe in* 'free will'. Since reality is at its heart an impenetrable mystery, and since we cannot in practice see what are the distal causes of our proximal activities, we are almost bound to become focused on the *experience* of the processes of action as we are bodily engaged in them. These processes are, furthermore, a *necessary* part of our experience, and cannot be disregarded. It is, in fact, not possible to be 'fatalistic' and to sit back as, so to speak, a spectator while the powers of determinism take over, pushing us around like puppets. For there is no entity 'inside' us capable of spectating; whether we like it or not, we are 'fated' to be actively complicit in our fate! While we cannot in effect pit our will against the distal powers which flow through us, we also cannot but experience them as the workings of our will.

It is only at times of acute conflict and distress that the paradoxes implicit in the idea of 'will' make themselves felt. We do not normally find it difficult to distinguish between actions we are happy to perform and ones which we feel constrained to carry out 'against our will', but there are times when actions of a kind which usually fit into the former category fall into the latter, and it is at such times that we may catch a glimpse of the inadequacy of our everyday ways of thinking about these things. There's nothing like trying to diet, or break free of an addiction like smoking, to demonstrate how fragile is the concept of 'will'. In the normal course of daily events, however, we are easily enough lulled into the belief that our co-operation with distal power (so long as it appears to coincide with our interests) is our own free choice.

*

We shall, therefore, not be able to change the world purely through an act of will, however clearly we might see the desirability of doing so. Even less shall we be able to make our lives any more comfortable through the cultivation of therapeutic make-believe.

What confronts us is a political programme in which an ethics built on reason and a knowledge of the world inspired by faith in its reality enable us to reconstruct 'forms' which can earn the assent of people secure enough to appreciate their worth. Even though our present social organization gives rise to enough distress to underline the desirability of such a programme, it may well be the case that the causes of such distress still appear too abstract and ideologically obscured to provide the necessary impetus for change.

When enough people hurt badly enough to be moved to act together against the roots of our troubles, one can only hope that they may be in a better position than has often been the case before to know what to do.

Appendix

What follows gives a summary of the theoretical position outlined in this book, relating particularly closely to the text of Chapter Three (figure 3, page 74, in that chapter offers a similar, though rather more simplified, summary in diagrammatic form).

I have thus set out here what seem to me the principal features of an 'environmental' approach to human distress in the form of simple statements which I would regard as fundamental. Where there is adequate explanation of these statements in the main text, I have left them here unelaborated. Where there are points of emphasis to be made, or where some further clarification may be needed, I have added some brief notes.

FUNDAMENTALS OF AN ENVIRONMENTAL APPROACH TO DISTRESS

1 A person is the interaction of a body with a world (environment).

The important point to grasp here is that there are no 'things' involved in the construction of personhood other than bodies and worlds. A person is not a thing, but an interaction; anything *material* about a person is either body or world. There is no particular harm in calling nonmaterial aspects of the person 'mind', or even 'spirit'; difficulties arise only when such concepts are subtly rematerialized and regarded as 'inside' the person in some semiphysical sense (it is no doubt also confusions of this kind that lead to conceptions of 'immortal souls' which are somehow inseparable from mysteriously resurrectable bodies).

2 By 'environment' is meant, most importantly, social space-time.

3 The environment is structured by material power.

4 Power may be coercive, economic or ideological. These may be, but are not necessarily, positively correlated.

5 Ideological power is viable only to the extent that it can be rendered material through solidarity.

Statements 3, 4 and 5 attempt to express the idea that power is exerted *physically* on the world through human action, and that its operation can be inferred only through the observation of *material* change having taken place in physical structures. Ideological power can be effective only through its association with material force of this kind. 'Ideas', of themselves, have no power; what makes the difference between magic and wishful thinking on the one hand and ideologies like Christianity or Nazism on the other is that the latter are empowered through the association of large numbers of people able to *act* together.

6 The person's relation to the body is mainly one of sensation.

7 The person's relation to the environment is mainly through experience (intransitive reception of power) and action (transitive exercise of power).

A person is thus located in a field of power which s/he both absorbs and transmits, and from which s/he cannot be abstracted as an individual able somehow to choose or decide how to relate to the field of power independently of its influence. Our experience of being permeated by social power necessarily imparts the illusion that we *originate* action, but, in fact, we would more accurately be characterized as *loci* in social space *through which* power flows. (See 20 and 21 below.)

8 Both the experience and the exercise of power may be benign or malign.

That is to say, social influences may operate for or against the interests of the person they impinge upon, and s/he may in turn act for or against the interests of others. What a person believes about these processes (whether s/he perceives influences as malign or benign; whether s/he is 'sincere' about the 'motives' for his/her actions) is not essential to an accurate understanding of them, and may indeed be controlled by ideological powers of which the person has no knowledge.

9 Power operates at varying distance from the person – proximally and distally. It is always mediated proximally, but may well originate distally.

10 a From an objective perspective, the absolute magnitude of power is negatively related to its proximity to the person.
  b From a subjective perspective, the relative magnitude of power is positively related to its proximity to the person.

11 Each person operates within: a) a 'power horizon', and b) a 'memory span' which limits his/her ability to identify the reasons for proximal events and actions, including his/her own.

Between them, 9, 10 and 11 contain perhaps the most difficult and profound paradox of human experience. This is that, in trying to understand the reasons for social conduct, including his/her own, what are in fact the *least* accurate and satisfactory explanations are likely to be experienced by the individual as the *most* accurate and satisfactory ones. The person thus comes to live within a kind of illusory mythology which can be corrected only by a more 'objective' view, i.e., one which inhabits a much broader power horizon (it is just such a correction which the natural sciences attempt to perform for our understanding of the physical world). The 'truth' could, in any absolute sense, only be seen through the eye of God, but any version of it to which human beings can aspire, however extended their power horizon, can only be an approximation. It is essentially this paradox of human experience which makes the operation of ideological mystification – 'false consciousness', or simple 'bamboozlement' – possible.

12 **Environmental influence becomes embodied (i.e., becomes a collection of biological assets and liabilities).** Whether environmental influence permeates the person intransitively or flows through him/her transitively, it is physically registered, materially changing physical structures such that learning can take place. Learning is thus inescapably a biological process and may well be irreversible.

13 **There are no such things as 'inner worlds', but personal powers acquired (embodied) over time.**

14 **The extent to which a person can influence present circumstances will depend on the availability to him/her of material powers and resources, including embodied personal assets.**

15 **Powers and resources may be economic, cultural, educational, ideological, physical.**

16 **The degree to which the effects of the past can be influenced will depend on the nature and extent of their embodiment as well as on the person's access to resources.**

17 **A person's 'psychology' consists of the meaning systems through and with which his/her embodied experience of the environment is understood, interpreted and represented.** That we arrive at 'psychology' only at this point suggests some of its limitations. For psychology deals essentially with an abstracted *relation* of bodies with worlds, with that aspect of people which is neither body nor world, and which reflects their struggles to represent and talk about what it is like to be a body in a world. Perhaps this is why so many psychologists who pursue their speculations with any real tenacity tend to end up either as quasi-biologists or quasi-sociologists. The great temptation for psychology is, of course, to impute to its insights (into the systems

of meaning people develop to understand their world) a materiality they simply haven't got, and then to attempt to tie such *pseudo*material insights into *truly* material aspects of bodies and worlds. The most obvious example of this is to assume in one form or another the power of positive (or indeed negative) thinking, to try to make *direct* and *causal* connections between the way we see things and the way they are. *Of course* we cannot separate the way things are from the way we see them, but nor can we create a world just by imagining it. The importance of understanding a person's meaning-systems is for the clues it gives us to body-world relations; we change nothing of consequence by trying simply to manipulate those systems from within themselves. A more technical way of saying this is to point out that psychology confuses epistemological observations with ontological statements.

18 Such meaning systems may be, for example, idiosyncratic or cultural, implicit or explicit.
Even such simple distinctions as these, which may be represented on two orthogonal axes as shown, can give a theoretical coherence to psychological phenomena which if treated as entities in 'internal space' tend to multiply perplexingly. The schema here owes a great deal to the work of Rom Harré (see his *Personal Being*, Blackwell, 1983).

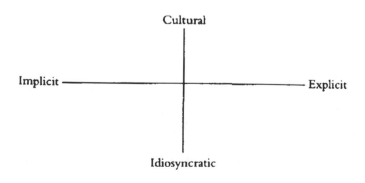

According to this schema, the character of a psychological phenomenon will be determined by its location relative to the two axes of meaning. For example a scientific production, and indeed language itself, would be found in the upper right quadrant, while some artistic productions (making explicit an idiosyncratic view) would be in the lower right quadrant; dreaming, and some forms of psychotic ideation, would be located mainly in the lower left quadrant. 'Symptoms' of distress which are commonly experienced but which people are at a loss to understand might find their place in the upper left quadrant. An example of one of these latter might be 'anorexia' (the meaning of self-starvation is almost certainly culturally determined, but remains mysteriously inarticulate; inasmuch as it becomes articulated as a form of protest – hunger strike – it moves along to the right of the horizontal axis).

By means such as these, the curious mixed metaphors of 'dynamic' psychology – for example, the hydraulics of 'internal' space in which 'mental contents' are pushed into and out of consciousness – may be replaced by *conceptual* distinctions giving, at a meta-level, coherence to phenomena which, insofar as they are purely psychological, are themselves conceptual (i.e., aspects of meaning-systems).

It is important to note that psychological phenomena are not necessarily unique or private to the individual in whom they occur (i.e., who provides a locus for them), but may be aspects of cultural 'forms' established independently of specific individuals.

19 Psychological operations may effect change only to the extent that they directly mediate, or facilitate access to, powers and resources.

20 The concept of 'will' derives from the *experience* of transmitting power, provided such transmission is congruent with the individual's wishes.

21 Freedom is proportional to the amount of power possessed by or available to the individual.

The idea that we have 'free will' thus derives from the experience most of us have had of being able to exercise a certain amount of power. Because we are especially intimately acquainted with the sensations of our own bodies (and may well be ignorant of the source and nature of the powers we sometimes transmit), we mistakenly identify the feelings which accompany the exercise of power as its origination, and we call this 'will'. Since we cannot choose not to have such feelings, it seems reasonable to suggest that 'will' is a *necessary* illusion.

22 A person's wellbeing (freedom from distress) is largely determined by current circumstances and the nature and significance of his/her embodied experience and exercise of power.

The interaction of the characteristics of power – whether it is benign or malign, transitive or intransitive – together with their mediation through the person's systems of meaning will determine whether the person feels pleasure or pain, love or hate, comfort or distress, confidence or fear, etc. For example, power exercised by the person transitively and benignly is likely to be experienced as loving, transitively but malignly as sadistic. Similarly, the intransitive reception of benign power is likely to be experienced as being loved, and so on.

The mediation of experience and action by the person's 'psychology' (meaning-systems) is important *not* because it can be 'therapeutically' manipulated to change distress into comfort (which in most cases would amount merely to ideological distortion or mystification), but because engagement with it offers opportunities for the clarification of previous distortions and mystifications (as well as, of course, for learning from the person what s/he knows about the world).

23 Clinical consultation ('therapy') operates only transiently within the person's proximal field and is therefore necessarily limited in its power to effect change.

24 Consultation consists of three main elements:
   (i) provision of comfort
   (ii) clarification
   (iii) encouragement in the use of available powers and
   resources.

Index

Printed in the United States
by Baker & Taylor Publisher Services